P9-CDE-737

Break Those Chains at Last

AFRICAN AMERICANS
1860–1880

THE YOUNG OXFORD HISTORY OF
AFRICAN AMERICANS

Robin D. G. Kelley and Earl Lewis
General Editors

Break Those Chains at Last

◇ ◇ ◇

AFRICAN AMERICANS
1860–1880

NORALEE FRANKEL

Oxford University Press
New York • Oxford

To Elizabeth Jennifer Frankel Kost and William E. Kost

Author's note: The primary sources for this book included interviews with former slaves collected in the 1930s by the Works Progress Administration (WPA). Although most of these interviews were not recorded, the interviewers often transcribed their notes with an attempt at re-creating Southern dialect.

Oxford University Press

Oxford New York
Athens Auckland Bangkok Bombay
Calcutta Cape Town Dar es Salaam Delhi
Florence Hong Kong Istanbul Karachi
Kuala Lumpur Madras Madrid Melbourne
Mexico City Nairobi Paris Singapore
Taipei Tokyo Toronto
and associated companies in
Berlin Ibadan

Published by Oxford University Press, Inc.
198 Madison Avenue, New York, New York 10016

Oxford is a registered trademark of Oxford University Press

Library of Congress Cataloging-in-Publication Data

Frankel, Noralee
Break those chains at last: African Americans, 1860–1880 / Noralee Frankel.
p. cm. — (The Young Oxford history of African Americans; vol. 5)
Includes bibliographical references and index.
1. United States—History—Civil War, 1861–1865—Afro-Americans—Juvenile literature. 2. Afro-Americans—History—
To 1863—Juvenile literature. 3. Slaves—United States—Emancipation—Juvenile literature. 4. Afro-Americans—
History—1863–1877—Juvenile literature. [1. Afro-Americans—History—19th century.]
I. Title. II. Series.
E540.N3F73 1995
305.896'073'009034—dc20
95-1848
CIP
AC

ISBN 0-19-508798-4; ISBN 0-19-508502-7 (series)

1 3 5 7 9 8 6 4 2

Printed in the United States of America
on acid-free paper

Design: Sandy Kaufman
Layout: Loraine Machlin
Picture research: Lisa Kirchner, Laura Kreiss

On the cover: A recruitment poster for the Union army.
Frontispiece: A Southern street scene, probably in Richmond, Virginia, after the end of Reconstruction.
Page 9: Detail from *The Contribution of the Negro to Democracy in America* (1943), by Charles White, 11'9" x 17'3".
Hampton University Museum, Hampton, Virginia.

CONTENTS

◇ ◇ ◇

ROBIN D.G. KELLEY
EARL LEWIS

INTRODUCTION

The years of civil war and reconstruction challenged the very foundations of American democracy and established the place of African Americans in that democracy. The war raised the intriguing question of whether a state or collection of states had the right to leave the Union when residents felt their way of life was under attack. It eventually raised the question of whether a nation founded on the deep belief in freedom could deny those same rights and privileges to others because of differences in color and status. Fundamentally, the years bounded by the Civil War and Reconstruction raised extremely important questions about the place of African Americans in a newly reconstructed nation.

When Southern forces fired on Fort Sumter, South Carolina, in 1861, sparking a confrontation between the federal government and the Southern states, the end of a way of life was at hand. The country had grown increasingly polarized over the issue of slavery. Some people favored total abolition; others simply wished to contain slavery, halting its further spread. Yet, after the war's start and despite the pleas of such prominent African Americans as Frederick Douglass, President Abraham Lincoln and members of Congress hesitated to make slavery the central issue of the struggle. Initially, Lincoln sought simply to reunite the country. But with growing pressures from some whites, and in light of black agitation, the freedom of African Americans became a paramount concern.

The emancipation of slaves and the abolition of slavery was neither immediate nor universally applied. And the shift from slavery to freedom

First graders in Greenville, South Carolina, around 1880. Gaining an education was one way for blacks to take control of their lives after the Civil War.

introduced a number of searching questions for Southern blacks. Although the majority favored freedom over enslavement, a few feared such a dramatic change in status. Many, for example, ran away to join army units, where they encountered Northern blacks heading south to aid in their liberation. Others filled the contraband camps—so called because fleeing slaves had no legal status and were considered contraband—that flanked Northern encampments. And even after Lincoln signed the Emancipation Proclamation in 1863, blacks living in border states such as West Virginia were not freed until passage of the 13th Amendment to the Constitution in 1865. Still, a few served in the Confederate army, which is not surprising because a few blacks had been slave owners.

When the war ended in 1865, many African Americans anticipated their inclusion in the nation's civic culture. With ratification of the 14th Amendment (1868), which granted blacks citizenship, and the 15th (1870), which gave black men the right to vote, they were free and optimistic. Scores searched anxiously for family members sold during slavery; others exercised their right to form labor associations and to build schools, churches, and other institutions. Families withdrew women and children from the labor force, thereby asserting a right to be treated as paid, free labor. Continued racial violence tempered some of this optimism, of course. Race riots, lynchings, forced labor, and other legal and illegal methods persisted. Nonetheless, blacks voted and played an active role in the affairs of the nation. This book explains how African Americans finally broke the chains of bondage and participated in the reconstruction of the nation.

This book is part of an 11-volume series that narrates African-American history from the 15th through the 20th centuries. Since the 1960s, a rapid explosion in research on black Americans has significantly modified previous understanding of that experience. Studies of slavery, African-American culture, social protest, families, and religion, for example, silenced those who had previously labeled black Americans insignificant historical actors. This new research followed a general upsurge of interest in the social and cultural experiences of the supposedly powerless men and women who did not control the visible reins of power. The result has been a careful and illuminating portrait of how ordinary people make history and serve as the architects of their own destinies.

This series explores many aspects of the lives of African Americans. It describes how blacks shaped and changed the history of this nation. It also places the lives of African Americans in the context of the Americas as a whole. We start the story more than a century before the day in 1619 when 19 "negars" stepped off a Spanish ship in Jamestown, Virginia, and end with the relationship between West Indian immigrants and African Americans in large urban centers like New York in the late 20th century.

At the same time, the series addresses a number of interrelated questions: What was life like for the first Africans to land in the Americas, and what were the implications for future African Americans? Were all Africans and African Americans enslaved? How did race shape slavery and how did slavery influence racism? The series also considers questions about male-female relationships, the forging of African-American communities, religious beliefs and practices, the experiences of the young, and the changing nature of social protest. The key events in American history are here, too, but viewed from the perspective of African Americans. The result is a fascinating and compelling story of nearly five centuries of African-American history.

THE YOUNG OXFORD HISTORY OF
AFRICAN AMERICANS

"Go Down Moses"

When Israel was in Egypt's land,
Let my people go,
Oppressed so hard they could not stand,
Let my people go.

Go Down, Moses,
Way down in Egypt's land,
Tell old Pharaoh to
Let my people go!

"Thus saith the Lord," bold Moses said,
Let my people go,
"If not I'll smite your first-born dead,"
Let my people go.

No more shall they in bondage toil,
Let my people go,
Let them come out with Egypt's spoil,
Let my people go.

We need not always weep and mourn,
Let my people go,
And wear those slavery chains forlorn,
Let my people go.

The devil thought he had us fast,
Let my people go,
But we thought we'd break those chains at last,
Let my people go.

CHAPTER 1

CIVIL WAR: "WE HAVE DONE A SOLDIERS DUTY"

◇ ◇ ◇

Alfred Thomas was a slave in Mississippi when he first encountered the Union army. After Union soldiers rescued a slave from the plantation where Thomas lived, he and his companions decided that they wanted to escape slavery by going with the Yankees. As he recalled years after the Civil War, in 1898:

> Well we had been hearing the guns at Natchez and all over the country and everybody was scared and kept hearing people say the negroes would be free and we heard of colored people running off to the Yankees and one day the Yankees came to our place and took Henry Farron, a slave on the place and who was at the time bound in irons because he had run away. [The Union soldiers went] over to the blacksmith shop and cut the irons off of him and burned the smoke-house open and took all the molasses they wanted and then took Henry Farron off with them. This made us think more than ever about running off to the army. So about two or three days before we left, we had positively decided to go. We had arranged it all as we worked along in the field. [Several men decided to go together when] my master was at the home of his brother that night. . . . So we all went to the lot and killed a nice shoat and carried him up in the woods and broiled him up good and then bush-whacked it right in to Natchez, Miss. We traveled all night long and reached Natchez early the following morning. [The soldiers sent them by boat to Vicksburg.] That day and night we laid at a tent and rest and the following day they took us to a room there and stripped us naked and the doctors examined us one by one to see if we were fit for soldiers.

The 107th U.S. Colored Infantry at Fort Corcoran, near Washington, D.C., during the Civil War. "One black regiment alone," according to Frederick Douglass, "would be . . . the full equal of two white ones. The very fact of color in this case would be more terrible than powder and balls."

13

Alfred Thomas was one of 180,000 African Americans who served in the Union army during the Civil War. Some 29,000 black men also fought in the Union navy. African Americans participated in 52 engagements, at a cost of 37,000 lives.

While African-American men contributed to the war effort as a fighting force, African-American women's labor also supported the Union cause. Women who escaped to the Union soldiers were placed on Union-controlled plantations. These women, along with men not fit for military service, raised cotton; the profits were used in the war effort. This was the first large-scale experiment in free labor in the South. The struggle of these men and women to free themselves and their attempts to define freedom during and after the war are the major themes in the story of African Americans during the Civil War and Reconstruction.

Slavery had existed in the United States for almost two centuries before the Civil War. As a combined legal, social, economic, and ideological institution, it ultimately caused the Civil War.

The first Africans introduced into colonial Virginia were most likely treated as indentured servants—that is, they were required to work for someone else for a specified period of time. But sometime between 1673 and 1698, slavery based on race appeared. Certainly by 1700, Africans had become permanent enslaved laborers, and they passed that inferior status to their children, even if one parent was European.

Slavery existed in both the North and South, although it ended in the North long before the Civil War. With agricultural and manufacturing changes, slavery grew in the South during the first part of the 19th century. The cotton gin allowed for the mechanical removal of seeds out of cotton, which meant that it could be processed more quickly. Improved strains of hybrid cotton were developed by crossbreeding different types; the hybrids were easier to pick and more resistant to disease. As cotton production became dominant in the South, the use of slaves increased. With the aid of the U.S. government, white settlers pushed Indians off their land, and more slave owners moved from the upper South to the lower Southern states further west, such as Mississippi and Texas.

The majority of slave men, women, and children worked as agricultural laborers in the South. Slaves often did the work of growing cotton, tobacco, or rice on plantations, the large farms organized around slave

These contrabands ran to Union forces in Williamsport, Virginia, in 1862. Often, women and those men unable to fight were put to work on Union-controlled plantations.

labor. On cotton plantations, for example, slaves prepared the soil by plowing, then planted the seed, hoed the fields to keep out weeds, and picked the cotton. In the North before the abolition of slavery and in the South, slaves also worked on small farms whose masters owned only one or two slaves.

Enslaved men and woman also performed nonagricultural work. In the South, where the vast majority of slaves labored, slave women in cities worked as domestics in private homes or sold fruits and vegetables in open markets. Enslaved men in urban areas worked as butlers and as personal servants to white men in private houses. Slave men also built ships, smelt iron, did carpentry work, and labored in tobacco factories.

In the North during the prewar years, a movement to abolish slavery grew. Prominent African-American abolitionists included both free African Americans in the North, such as James Forten, a wealthy sailmaker and inventor, and his family in Philadelphia, and runaway or newly freed slaves such as Frederick Douglass and Sojourner Truth. Douglass was an extraordinarily powerful speaker about the horrors of slavery, and he edited an antislavery newspaper. Through lectures, lobbying, and writing, white and African-American abolitionists agitated for outlawing slavery, even though they were occasionally the victims of mob violence.

Frederick Douglass was an eloquent abolitionist who remembered that as a child, he was "strongly impressed with the idea of being a free man some day."

Although most Northerners were not abolitionists, they became increasingly uneasy as slavery moved west in the 1830s and 1840s into states such as Texas. Northerners, both farmers and those who worked for wages, were afraid that free (non-slave) labor could not compete with slavery and that non-slaveholders would lose political and economic power within the country as slavery expanded. At the same time in the South, slave owners and other white Southerners became convinced that citizens had a right to own slaves. Southern leaders argued that individual states, rather than the federal government, had the authority to decide whether a state should allow slavery or not. After failed slave rebellions in 1822 and 1831 and other appeals calling for slaves to revolt, Southern legislatures restricted access to antislavery materials and severely limited debates on the abolition of slavery. Such actions upset Northerners concerned about preserving free speech, and they began to perceive the South as a closed and undemocratic society.

Starting with the debates over the writing of the U.S. Constitution in the late 1780s, politicians struggled with the issue of slavery. When a new state entered the Union, congressmen argued over whether that state would allow slavery or not. In 1819, Missouri applied to Congress for admission to the Union as a slave state. In a series of compromises, collectively known as the Missouri Compromise or the Compromise of 1820, Missouri was allowed to enter as a slave state and Maine was allowed to enter as a free state. Congress prohibited slavery in all other territory north of Missouri's southern boundary (the 36th parallel), and Missouri was permitted to keep a statute in its state constitution that forbade free African Americans from settling there. In 1849, as more territories wanted to become states, Congress was again beset by troubling issues involving slavery and the right of states to make decisions without interference from the federal government. In 1850, Congressman Henry Clay offered several resolutions that ultimately made up the Compromise of 1850. These included admitting California to the Union as a free state, allowing slavery in the territory gained from the war with Mexico, abolishing the slave trade in the District of Columbia, and passing a stricter federal fugitive slave law. These last two items were part of the compromise because Northerners had objected to the auctioning of African Americans in the nation's capital and Southerners had been increasingly frustrated by the lack of help from Northern officials in regaining their runaway slaves. The 1850 Fugitive Slave Law was vehemently opposed in the North, however. Groups of Northerners, both blacks and whites, tried to rescue runaway slaves to prevent their forced return to the South. Some runaways living peacefully in the North for years fled to Canada rather than risk recapture.

Meanwhile, the country was becoming increasingly polarized over slavery, and the North and South became suspicious of each other's political power. Slavery was tied to the fight over states' rights—the doctrine that all rights not reserved to the federal government by the

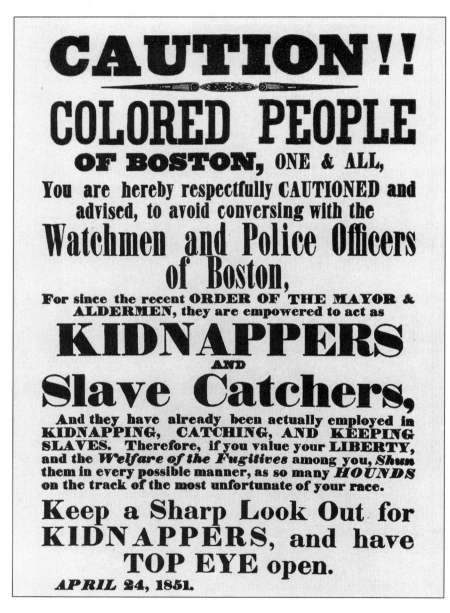

CAUTION!!
COLORED PEOPLE
OF BOSTON, ONE & ALL,

You are hereby respectfully CAUTIONED and advised, to avoid conversing with the

Watchmen and Police Officers of Boston,

For since the recent ORDER OF THE MAYOR & ALDERMEN, they are empowered to act as

KIDNAPPERS
AND
Slave Catchers,

And they have already been actually employed in KIDNAPPING, CATCHING, AND KEEPING SLAVES. Therefore, if you value your LIBERTY, and the *Welfare of the Fugitives* among you, *Shun* them in every possible manner, as so many *HOUNDS* on the track of the most unfortunate of your race.

Keep a Sharp Look Out for KIDNAPPERS, and have TOP EYE open.
APRIL 24, 1851.

This 1851 poster warns blacks in Boston to beware of the Fugitive Slave Law, which provided for the recapture and return of slaves who escaped to the North.

U.S. Constitution are granted to the states. Disputes between the supporters of slavery and the proponents of free labor were responsible for many of the political, economic, cultural, and ideological differences.

In 1854, as in the Missouri Compromise of 1820, the admittance of new states to the Union led to conflict in Congress. The compromise ultimately led to bloodshed in the newly established territories. Congress suggested that the Kansas and Nebraska territories be allowed to exercise self-determination rather than making them abide by the Missouri Compromise. The territories themselves would then decide, through their legislatures, whether they would enter the country as slave or free states. Rather than avoiding conflict, this compromise, the Kansas-Nebraska Act, precipitated violence. In 1855, fighting between proslavery advocates and abolitionists broke out over the issue of slavery in Kansas. "Bleeding Kansas," as it became known, was a portent of the Civil War. Another was John Brown's raid in Harpers Ferry, Virginia. After fighting in Kansas for the antislavery forces, John Brown, who was white, led a group of African Americans and whites to Virginia in 1859 to try to inspire a slave rebellion. The plan failed and Brown was hanged, but many Northerners applauded his actions.

When Abraham Lincoln ran for President in 1860, many Southerners assumed he wanted to abolish slavery. Lincoln did oppose any further spread of slavery, but he did not, in fact, intend to end the practice. Nevertheless, upon Lincoln's election, legislatures of states in the South seceded from the United States by declaring that the states were no longer part of the Union. First, South Carolina seceded on December 20, 1864, followed by Mississippi, Florida, Alabama, Georgia, Louisiana, Texas, Virginia, North Carolina, Arkansas, and Tennessee. These eleven states joined together to form the Confederate States of America. They elected their own President, Jefferson Davis, and after initial debate established a capital in Richmond, Virginia.

Fighting began between the Union and Confederate supporters over Fort Sumter, in the harbor of Charleston, South Carolina. After demanding that the U.S. Army surrender the fort, Confederate soldiers fired at it, and on April 14, 1861, Fort Sumter surrendered to the Confederacy. This event marked the beginning of formal hostilities between the North and the South.

The Confederacy proceeded to organize an army under the leadership of Robert E. Lee. A West Point graduate and trained officer, Lee had turned down President Lincoln's offer to command the Union troops. Failing to obtain Lee, Lincoln named George McClellan general of the Union forces. But Lincoln grew frustrated by McClellan's cautiousness and failure to pursue the enemy. He replaced McClellan with a succession of generals to head the Union forces but found them all unsatisfactory. Lincoln finally selected General Ulysses S. Grant to head the Union's forces because he had proved to be an aggressive, tenacious fighter. Grant's fearlessness ultimately resulted in far greater casualties than would have occurred under McClellan, but under Grant's leadership the Union army won the war.

For the first two years of the war, Lincoln justified the fighting only as necessary to save the United States from becoming two separate countries. Not wanting to antagonize the border states like Kentucky and Missouri, which were slave states that had stayed in the Union, Lincoln refused to deal with the slave issue in any systematic manner. As the war progressed, however, African Americans and white abolitionists pushed Lincoln to change his mind and add the elimination of slavery to the reasons the Union was fighting the Civil War.

Free African Americans as well as slaves were convinced much earlier than Lincoln that a Northern victory would end slavery, even though the stated purpose of the war was to save the Union. As Frederick Douglass, a noted abolitionist, orator, and journalist, explained, "The American people and the Government at Washington may refuse to recognize it for a time but the 'inexorable logic of events' will force it upon them in the end; that the war now being waged in this land

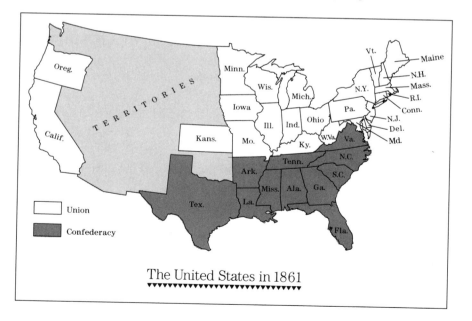

The United States in 1861

President Lincoln meets with Union officers in 1862, after the Battle of Antietam. Although Lincoln claimed that the purpose of the war was to save the Union, rather than to end slavery, he had declared during his 1858 campaign for the Senate, "I believe this Government cannot endure permanently half slave and half free."

is a war for and against slavery." One African American complained, "Our union friends says the[y] are not fighting to free the negroes . . . we are fighting for the union . . . very well let the white fight for what the[y] want and we negroes fight for what we want . . . liberty must take the day." Dora Franks, a young domestic slave who overheard the whites in her household mention the war, recounted that she "started prayin' for freedom and all the rest of de women did the same thing."

During the war, some slaves remained on the plantation while others, for a variety of reasons, escaped to the Union lines. Some planters fled to Texas and other states to keep their slaves away from the Union army. These flights made slave escapes almost impossible. When the soldiers were nearby, male slaves could escape but elderly slaves and women with small children often found it difficult to run to Union lines. As slaves fled, the work of those who remained on the plantation expanded. As one man recalled, during the war, slave owners made slave children "do a man's work." One 15-year-old girl recalled that she "plowed a mule an' a wild un at dat. Sometimes me hand get so cold I jes' cry."

Raids on a plantation by soldiers—of both armies—increased the difficulty of the slaves' work. For example, at one plantation soldiers carried off grain and most of the livestock, so the African Americans who remained lacked sufficient food. Fortunately, in this case the shrewdness of the slaves prevented the soldiers from getting the turkeys. The slaves had sprinkled corn underneath the house, and when the turkeys wandered there to eat it, the slaves penned them in and destroyed their tracks. Although such resourcefulness did save some food, deprivations caused by the war affected both the Southern whites and the African Americans on plantations. Slaves who remained on plantations after soldiers' rampages recalled that they "were all hungry many a time" during the war. Both Confederate and Union soldiers raided the slaves' quarters, taking their few possessions.

Harsh treatment by Union soldiers made some slaves wary of them. Moreover, if slaves helped the Northern soldiers, they could be punished by their masters once the soldiers left. Some slaves therefore failed to cooperate, to protect themselves. Once when a Union soldier confronted a slave woman and demanded to know where the silverware was hidden, she told him that her owners were too cheap to buy anything that nice. (She had earlier helped bury the silver near the very spot where she was speaking to the soldier.) However, many other slaves did not protect their masters' property from soldiers. As one white woman wrote bitterly in her journal after discovering that the Yankees had captured the family valuables, "Our old cook, who had been the most indulged and well treated servant imaginable, had betrayed their hiding place."

In this cartoon, slaves abandon their master and run to Fort Monroe. General Benjamin Butler, who was in command of that Virginia fort, had declared such runaways "contraband" and allowed them to stay with the Union forces.

The taking of food by Union soldiers and their destruction of plantation property confused some slaves, especially children. They developed an ambivalence toward the Union soldiers, unable to decide if the Yankees were their liberators or merely new enslavers. Even before having contact with them, slave children were predisposed to be afraid of Yankee soldiers because they had heard Southern whites refer to them as devils and monsters. Some slave children interpreted these words literally. Mollie Williams later recalled, "Us all thought de Yankees was some kin' of debils an' we was skeered to death of 'em." As a little girl, former slave Jan McLeod Wilburn fantasized that Yankees consisted only of "heads without bodies." One white overseer terrorized children by telling them that "a Yankee was sompin what had one great big horn on he haid and just one eye and dat right in de middle of the beast." When it came, the actual fighting also frightened the slave children. Decades later one freedwoman remembered that "when dose bombs began to fly an' de cannon go 'Boon boom' I wuz skeered to death." Another freedwoman explained, "The sound was like eternity had turned loose. Everything shook like terrible earthquakes day and night. The light was bright and red and smoke terrible."

Fear of the Union soldiers did not mean, however, that the slaves who remained on the plantations supported slavery or continued to work and act as they had under slavery. The Civil War and the general turmoil it brought destroyed the customary white authority on most plantations and small farms. As a result, slaves often refused to do certain kinds of work and argued over matters of discipline and the management of the plantation. Even before emancipation, they began to assert their rights as freed people. Before the close of the war, one slave owner greeted one of his workers with "Howdy, Uncle," but the slave responded with a demand for proper respect: "Call me Mister." On a minority of plantations, the freed slaves became violent, burning property and looting from their previous owners. Because of the war, some owners simply abandoned their plantations. The slaves who stayed behind divided the land and property among themselves. They planted food crops and sometimes cotton to sell.

Other slaves left their plantations to escape slavery. In the South, all through the war thousands of slaves freed themselves by running to the Union lines. As one military chaplain described it, "Blacks illustrated

what the history of the world has rarely seen,—a slave population . . .
leaving its bondage of centuries . . . individually or in families. . . . Their
comings were like the arrivals of cities." Leaving one's family to seek
freedom behind the Yankee lines was difficult. When his father escaped,
Levi McLaurin's son recalled, "I was present when he left and I told him
goodbye. He said he would be back after us all." The son "saw men put
dogs on his tracks and heard dogs running after my father." Another
male slave joined McLaurin but turned back after three miles "because I
could not leave my family."

If freed people running toward the Union lines were caught by
their masters, they were whipped or even killed. One newly freed man,
John Boston, escaped to a regiment from Brooklyn that was stationed in
Virginia. Missing his still-enslaved wife, he wrote her: "My Dear wife It
is with grate joy I take this time to let you know Where I am[.] i am now
in Safety in the 14th Regiment of Brooklyn[.] this Day i can Adress you

*Whole families some-
times fled to the
Union lines, where
they hoped to find
freedom. The glass
plate negative of
this rare photo
was cracked.*

thank god as a free man[.] I had a little trouble in giting away." He added, "I trust the time Will Come When We Shal meet again[.] And if We dont met on earth We will Meet in heaven."

As the war progressed, more women, particularly if they did not have small children, accompanied the men. Former slave woman Maggie Dixon recalled that when "the Union cavalry came past our plantation, told us to quit work, and follow them, we were all too glad to do so." Slaves were especially eager to leave the plantations after soldiers destroyed the food supplies there.

At the beginning of the war, the federal government had no policy regarding the treatment of escaping slaves. However, the sheer number of fleeing slaves soon pushed Congress and the Union army into forming a plan to deal with the slaves' aspirations for freedom. As soon as the Union army approached, slaves from neighboring plantations ran to its lines, hoping for their freedom. But to the slaves' disappointment, Northern soldiers in the early part of the war returned runaway slaves to their masters. Not all the Yankee generals agreed with this policy. In May 1861, General Benjamin Butler, stationed in Virginia, declared the runaway slaves "contraband," or property taken during war, and allowed them to stay with the army. Butler later explained, "I was always a friend of southern rights, but an enemy of southern wrongs." Butler's policy of freeing individual slaves who escaped to the Union army was tolerated by the federal government. Nevertheless, when other Union generals issued more sweeping orders freeing all the slaves in territories under their command, President Lincoln overrode them.

To help clarify the status of the slaves, in August 1861 Congress passed the first Confiscation Act, which kept slave owners from reenslaving runaways. Union soldiers occasionally continued to act as slave catchers and forced escaped slaves to go back to their masters. Finally, in March 1862, Congress passed a law forbidding Union soldiers from returning escaped slaves. Then in July 1862, Congress passed the second Confiscation Act, which more broadly freed the slaves of any master helping the Confederacy. Together, these measures began slowly to change the focus of the war toward a struggle for liberation by the slaves.

Throughout the war, the Union army had the practical problem of what to do with all the people fleeing to it. The army quickly put the men to work as drivers, cooks, blacksmiths, and construction workers, but the women, children, and elderly were more difficult to employ. For the fleeing slaves, the military established areas called contraband camps, usually near Union encampments. These contraband camps were often overcrowded and unsanitary. Moreover, when the soldiers moved on to fight another battle, their departure jeopardized the safety of the freed people living in the camps. White Southerners sometimes raided the camps, killing or recapturing their former slaves. Still, African Americans often established lasting friendships while living in the camps. Josephine Wilson met Margaret Williams when they "were both corralled . . . by the federal soldiers and taken up to Youngs Point" in Louisiana. After Williams's husband's death, she and Wilson moved to Louisiana, where they still lived at the turn of the century.

The composition of the contraband camps changed after July 1862 when the federal government began to allow African-American men to serve in the Union army. Once the men left, the women, children, and men unable to serve remained. Afraid that civilian freed people were becoming too dependent on government aid in the camps, U.S. officials decided to put them to work. The military therefore removed slave women, children, and men unfit for military duty from the contraband camps and placed them on abandoned plantations. There they became part of the first major experiment with non-slave labor in the South. These plantations were run either by Northern white men or by Southern planters who had taken a loyalty oath. In many areas, the employers had to promise not to whip the freed workers or use physical punishments against them.

These free laborers were supposed to be paid, but often they received very low wages and sometimes got no compensation at all. Their labor contracts also contained many restrictions. Some required, for instance, that the workers carry passes when they left the plantations, in a system reminiscent of slavery. Also, food and clothing were usually in short supply. The women were charged for their food and that of their children. Compounding these problems, Confederates sometimes raided these plantations and reenslaved the workers.

By the end of 1862, the women typically stayed in contraband camps or on plantations as wage laborers on Union-controlled plantations, while African-American men served in the army. The North was

A contraband servant works at the headquarters of the Third Army. Many African-American men who served in the military performed noncombat labor.

slow to see the value of enlisting African Americans, whether slave or free. As soon as the war started in 1861, many white abolitionists and blacks lobbied for enlisting African-American men into the army. When African-American men in the North prepared for war and tried to enlist, army recruiters turned them away. As one man from Ohio wrote to the secretary of war, "We beg that you will receive one or more regiments (or companies) of the colored of the free States. . . . We are partly drilled and would wish to enter active service immediately. . . . To prove our attachment and our will to defend the government we only ask a trial." The federal government refused, however, because officials were afraid that white soldiers would not want to fight alongside blacks. As the war

dragged on, however, fewer white men wanted to serve in a war with such high casualties. As voluntary enlistments dropped off, the federal government instituted a draft that proved highly unpopular with many Northern whites. In July 1863 whites rioted against the draft in New York City, blaming African Americans for the war, and rampaged against them. Rioters murdered blacks and burned down an African-American orphanage and a church. The administrator of the orphanage managed to remove all the children to safety before the building was torched, however.

At this Union army hospital in Nashville, Tennessee, escaped slaves worked as cooks, laundresses, and nurses.

In July 1862, the government decided to allow African Americans to join the Union army. Although some of those who served in all-black regiments were free Northern blacks, such as Frederick Douglass's sons, most African-American soldiers were former Southern slaves. Many runaways chose to enlist, although some were given little choice by Union officers needing to make their quotas of recruits. Many former slaves joined the army in a group. As one soldier recollected: "Ever since I can remember I have known James Gray. Before the war we both belonged to the same man and we enlisted together in Co. M [U.S. Colored Heavy Artillery] and mustered out at the same time and all the time after the war up to his death."

Some former-slave soldiers were linked by kinship bonds. For example, John J. Johnson and his uncle "served together and tented and messed together till we were mustered out." A very young James Hubbard, barely in his teens, served in the army at the same time as his father. Lasting friendships also developed between men in the army,

During the draft riots in New York City in 1863, troops were called in to stop the violence. Disillusioned with the war, many Northerners took out their frustrations on blacks.

strengthened by the shared military experience. One soldier, Frank Jackson, met his friend James Johnson in the army. "I knew him all through our term of service," remembered Jackson. "My association with him was of such a character that I knew most if not all of his business matters."

African-American soldiers faced many more obstacles than white men in trying to join the army. According to one report, when a group of African-American men in Kentucky enlisted in the Union army, "a mob of young men . . . followed these black men from town, seized them and whipped them most unmercifully with cow hides." Afterward "they declared that 'negro enlistments should not take place.'" On occasion white men beat, whipped, and even killed African Americans who tried to join the Union army.

Although the army paid white soldiers $13 a month, African-American soldiers received only $10, with $3 deducted for their clothing allowance. In protest, African-American soldiers in the 54th Massachusetts Infantry refused to accept any money until Congress guaranteed them equal pay, which it did in 1864. As one corporal in the 54th pointed out to President Lincoln: "We have done a Soldiers Duty. Why cant we have a Soldiers pay?. . . We feel as though, our Country spurned us, now we are sworn to serve her." Soldiers were also concerned about what receiving less money meant for their families. As one African American worried, "Many of these people have Families to support and no other means of doing it than what they get in this way."

African Americans served in segregated regiments, and the government refused to allow them to become officers. Blacks resisted these unfair policies. As one African-American sergeant wrote, "All we ask is to give us a chance, and a position higher than an orderly sergeant, the same as white soldiers, and then you will see that we lack for nothing." The government finally reversed itself and allowed African Americans to become officers.

African-American soldiers often worked not as fighters but as laborers, digging trenches, building forts, setting up camps, burying dead soldiers, cleaning, picking up garbage in camp, and other noncombat labor. In addition, African Americans used poorer quality weapons than whites while in the service. They also often received poorer medical attention. As one white doctor confessed, "Very few surgeons will do precisely the same for blacks as they would for whites."

A cook prepares meals for the Army of the Potomac.

Occasionally, women were able to accompany their men into the army, if they became army washerwomen and cooks. As army widow Elizabeth Kane explained, "I was with him [her husband] in the army. I washed for him during his entire service in the army. . . . The officers let me live in a tent with my husband." And when he was 10 years old, Robert Paul, whose father served in the infantry and whose mother worked as a laundrywoman for the army, explained that he "stayed with my father at the barracks a good deal" and "was well known by all the Company men." Black women following the army tried to stay close to their male family members, but the army felt that the presence of families undermined army discipline, so women and children were occasionally forced out of the barracks. African-American soldiers resented that white officers kept their wives in their own barracks but often forbid African-American women from living with their men.

When they remained on their old plantations, wives of the African-American soldiers faced retaliation from their slave owners. As one wife expressed to her husband in a letter: "You do not know how bad I am treated. They are treating me worse and worse every day. Our child cries for you." The letter ended hopefully, though, with "do the best you can and do not fret too much for me for it wont be long before I will be free and then all we make will be ours." Receiving such letters caused mixed reactions. Some soldiers wanted to leave the army and rescue their families; others became more motivated to stay and fight for freedom.

Many Northern whites believed that slavery produced men too docile and cowardly to fight. Because of such prejudices some whites doubted that blacks had the competence to fight in an orderly military fashion. Once former slaves had fought as Union soldiers, however, the doubters quickly changed their minds. As one white newspaper reporter

The U.S. Colored Artillery practices gun drills. Forced to serve in segregated regiments, black men faced unfair treatment by the federal government. They were paid less than white soldiers and often used inferior weapons.

Christian Fleetwood, a sergeant major of the Fifth Colored Troops, Third Division, 18th Army Corps, was awarded the Congressional Medal of Honor in 1864. The government initially refused to let blacks become officers but later relented.

raved, "It is useless to talk any more about negro courage. The men fought like tigers, each and every one of them." Whites were surprised when African-American regiments fought bravely at Port Hudson and Milliken's Bend, Louisiana; Fort Wagner, South Carolina; and the Battle of the Crater, near Petersburg, Virginia. At Port Hudson in May and at Fort Wagner in September 1863, African-American troops battled fiercely against tremendous Confederate advantages. Union deaths from the battles ran as high as 40 percent. The battle at Milliken's Bend took place just 10 days after the one at Port Hudson. At first the Confederates seemed certain of victory. Outnumbered, the African Americans fought with bayonets in hand-to-hand combat against the Confederate charge. The Confederates could not defeat them. After initially falling back, the black troops held their line and the Confederates finally retreated.

At Big Black River in Mississippi (May 1863), under fire from Confederate soldiers, the African-American soldiers burned a railroad bridge the Confederates needed to bring in supplies. The soldiers also destroyed a section of railroad track. One general described the African-American soldiers: "Of this fight I can only say that men could not have behaved more bravely. I have seen white troops fight in twenty-seven battles and I never saw any fight better." Military strategists utilized African-American soldiers as an element of surprise in the opening charge against Confederate soldiers. Such maneuvers proved effective. As one Yankee officer later wrote, "I confess I am surprised at the dash and courage of these men."

The Confederate government tried to counteract the effectiveness of the African-American troops by threatening to refuse to grant them the status of prisoners of war if captured. It announced that captured African-American soldiers would be resold into slavery or perhaps even killed. This policy was calculated to increase the risk to African-American soldiers if they enlisted in the Union army. One general recalled that in one fight "such of the Colored Soldiers as fell into the hands of the Enemy during the battle were brutally murdered." Nevertheless, the Confederate government's refusal to recognize the rights of African-American prisoners did not deter the soldiers. One answered his commander's warning that "it may be slavery or Death to some of you today" by saying "Lieutenant, I am ready to die for Liberty." In July 1863, President Lincoln announced that he would not exchange Confederate soldiers for Union prisoners if African-American men were not treated the same as white prisoners of war.

Although some Confederate soldiers treated African Americans as legitimate prisoners of war, others were far more brutal. In April 1864, for instance, Confederate soldiers killed unarmed African Americans trying to surrender at Fort Pillow, Tennessee. This massacre became a symbol of Confederate brutality against African-American troops. One black New Yorker wrote to President Lincoln: "If the murder of the colored troops at Fort Pillow is not followed by prompt action on the part of our government, it may as well disband all its colored troops for no soldiers whom the government will not protect can be depended upon."

In spite of their own and their families' hardships, African Americans were proud of their wartime contributions. As one African-American soldier explained, "This was the biggest thing that ever happened in my life. I felt like a man with a uniform on and a gun in my hand." These soldiers fought for freedom for themselves and their families. As one African-American former grocer from Ohio expressed it, "If roasting on a bed of coals of fire would do away with the curse of slavery, I would be willing to be the sacrifice." Another former slave, in South Carolina, had begun working in a store and made what was for that time exceptionally good wages, up to $50 a week. "But," he declared, "I'm going to stop keeping store. I'm going to enlist as a private in the black regiment. How can I expect to keep my freedom if I'm not willing to fight for it. . . . Yes, I w'ld enlist if I were making a thousand dollars a week."

African-American men made up almost a quarter of the navy during the Civil War. One reason is that sailors did not have to contend with as much discrimination as soldiers. For example, the Confederate policy of not exchanging African-American soldiers for whites did not apply to

African-American seamen aboard the U.S.S. Vermont, *stationed off Hilton Head, South Carolina, in 1863. African-American men made up almost one-fourth of the navy during the Civil War.*

sailors. And because the ships of the time were too small to set up racially segregated facilities, blacks and whites worked, ate, and bunked in the same quarters. Particularly toward the end of the war, few ships sailed without African-American crew members. They even made up the majority of the crew on a few ships.

Besides serving as soldiers, former slaves also acted as spies for the Union army. They were able to maneuver in and out of Confederate lines with more ease than Northern white men could. Southerners rarely suspected African Americans of carrying out covert activities. For instance, former slave Harriet Tubman, who during the prewar period helped slaves escape from Maryland to the North, spied during the war for the Union. She went to South Carolina, where for three years she gathered information for the military by talking to slaves living in Confederate-held areas.

Slaves contributed, often unwillingly, to the Confederate war effort. They frequently accompanied their masters into Confederate army camps to serve as personal servants. The Confederate government used slave labor to build fortifications: they cut wood, dug foundations, and did carpentry work. Slave men also moved supplies. The army paid the masters for their slaves' services. A few African-American soldiers did

Near Charleston, South Carolina, four slaves, at left, cook a meal for the Confederate soldiers playing cards.

serve in the Confederate army. In New Orleans, free African Americans formed two regiments, not in defense of slavery but to defend their homes against Yankee attack. Once the North took control of New Orleans, however, many of these African-American Confederate soldiers went over to the Union army, revealing the tenuousness of their commitment to the Confederacy. In March 1865, a month before the Civil War ended, the Confederacy, in desperation, finally allowed African-American soldiers to fight in return for their freedom.

When the North's African-American soldiers marched into Richmond, Virginia, as the capital of the Confederacy surrendered, white Southerners must have recognized that the war had destroyed slavery forever. Thousands of slaves had freed themselves by crossing over the Union lines. African-American soldiers served their country proudly in the Civil War, and many died for the honor. For their part, African-American women and children, crowded into contraband camps, endured the war as best they could. Many also worked on plantations and became part of the Northern plan of freed labor that started during the war. The military policies regarding such labor influenced the working relationships between the freed people and their former owners during the period of Reconstruction that followed the war. The Civil War brought freedom to the nation's slaves, but just what this freedom would mean for the formerly enslaved people was unclear.

CHAPTER 2

FREEDOM: "TAKE YOUR FREEDOM, MY BROTHERS AND SISTERS"

◇ ◇ ◇

After President Lincoln issued the Emancipation Proclamation in September 1862, Union soldiers went to the plantations and announced the slaves' freedom. The newly freed people, who had long yearned for freedom, greeted the news with great excitement and much celebration. Interviewed during the 1930s, Harry Bridges vividly recalled the day when three federal cavalrymen rode onto Major Sartin's plantation in Mississippi, where as a boy, Bridges had been enslaved. While looking for Sartin, they chanced upon a group of slave women hoeing cotton. Going before the women, a slave man was helping loosen the soil by plowing. As Bridges described it, "The Yankees stopped their horses and the leader called to the old negro at the plow and asked for the owner of the place. . . . The soldiers then inquired of him who the negroes were working for and if they had been told that they were free." When the women overheard the soldiers, "knowing a change had taken place" they "rushed to the quarters telling the news to the other women and children." Sartin had refused to tell his slaves that they were free, but the Union soldiers "told them of their freedom. One negro woman who was unable to believe the news asked if they might leave the plantation at the moment to go where they wished and of course she was answered in the affirmative much to her surprise."

Freed slaves at Hilton Head, South Carolina, sort cotton on a plantation confiscated by Union troops. For doing the same work they formerly did as slaves, these black workers were paid 25 cents a day plus food.

The freeing of Major Sartin's slaves illustrates two important themes of the Reconstruction period. The first is that former slave owners and Southern whites generally resisted treating African Americans as free and no longer slaves. When they finally did reconcile themselves to the end of slavery, former owners never believed that African Americans were equal to and should be granted the same rights as whites. The second is that freed people had to define freedom for themselves, like the woman described above. Typical definitions of freedom often included living where one wanted and receiving payment for one's labor. One woman recalled in the 1930s that the freed people had expressed the desire to "do like dey please wid no boss over dem, an' den dey wanted to go places an' have no patroller ketch dem."

Gradually, the federal government began to plan for the former slaves becoming free. In September 1862, after the Union forces won at Antietam, Maryland, President Lincoln issued his Emancipation Proclamation, declaring freedom for the enslaved people in the Confederacy effective January 1, 1863. Lincoln deliberated for quite a while before changing the focus of the Civil War from a war to save the Union to one to end slavery. Although he personally opposed slavery, he had acted cautiously because of political considerations, fearing opposition from such loyal slave states as Maryland and Missouri. He favored gradual, compensated emancipation, with slave masters receiving payment if they voluntarily freed their slaves. Lincoln slowly began to agree with those who thought that the fastest way to break the South's resistance and end the war would be to free the slaves. He also wanted to preempt the possibility of Great Britain's entering the war on the side of the South, because England depended on the South's cotton. He believed that the antislavery sentiment in Great Britain would keep that country out of the Civil War if a Northern victory were to free the slaves.

Of course, thousands of former slaves had already freed themselves by taking refuge among the Union soldiers, and thousands more would follow them. Where African Americans were already free, they celebrated January 1, 1863, as Emancipation Day. In Washington, D.C., for instance, one freedwoman changed the lyrics of the song "Go Down, Moses" to "Go down, Abraham, away down in Dixie's land, Tell Jeff Davis to let my people go." Although the Emancipation Proclamation did not free slaves throughout the nation (specifically in the border states), it

Blacks celebrate Lincoln's Emancipation Proclamation. The proclamation helped change the war from one fought only to preserve the Union to one fought to free the slaves.

did declare freedom for those slaves in Confederate-held territory and it did allow Union solders in the future to liberate slaves, like Major Sartin's, wherever they found them.

As soon as the Civil War began, slaves—believing that the war would free them—traded information about the progress of the war and Union troop movements. As the noted African-American educator Booker T. Washington recalled, "Though I was a mere child during the preparations for the Civil War and during the war itself, I now recall the many late-at-night whispered discussions that I heard my mother and other slaves on the plantation indulge in." Washington added, "These discussions showed that they understood the situation, and that they kept themselves informed of events by what was termed the 'grapevine telegraph.'"

With emancipation, discussion among African Americans intensified as to their vision of life as freed men and women. In 1865, just

before the Civil War ended, 20 African-American ministers met in Savannah, Georgia, with Secretary of War Edwin Stanton and Union general William Tecumseh Sherman to consider the future of the newly freed people. When the ministers were asked about the meaning of freedom, one responded that "freedom, as I understand it, . . . is taking us from under the yoke of bondage, and placing us where we could reap the fruit of our labor, take care of ourselves and assist the Government in maintaining our freedom." When asked how the government could best assist freed people, one minister answered, "The way we can best take care of ourselves is to have land, and turn it and till it by our own labor."

The primary desire for independence expressed by the ministers was echoed by many freed people. "I had a kind master," one former slave explained, "but I didn't know but any time I might be sold away off, and when I found I could get my freedom, I was very glad; and I wouldn't go again, because now I am for myself."

Freed people held definite opinions about what freedom meant. For all, from the youngest to the oldest, it meant being allowed to live

Waiting to see what kind of life freedom will bring, blacks gather on a street in Richmond after the Confederate surrender. Ruined buildings are visible in the distance.

with their families without the threat of any of them being sold. Freed-woman Lucy Galloway recalled her former master talking about the block where slaves had been auctioned, telling his slaves that "dis block has parted many a mother and chile, husband and wife—brother and sister—but, now you is all free as I am." Another freedwoman recalled that after emancipation, "Ma an' pa wuz free to live together an' dat wuz a joyous day when we could all be together." Many freed people placed a high value on having their families remain together. Now, with freedom, one man declared, "I won't wake up some mornin' ter fin' dat my mammy or some ob de rest of my family am done sold." Another freedman reasoned, after his own mother and father had been separated by being sold, "I has got thirteen great gran' chilluns an' I know har dey ever' one am. In slavery times dey'd have been on de block long time ago."

Former slaves, like the ministers who met with Secretary Stanton, also interpreted freedom as being able to live where they chose, to own land, and to be paid for their labor. Freedom also meant being able to

In Vicksburg, Mississippi, a chaplain of the Freedmen's Bureau marries a black soldier and his bride. Being able to create and maintain family ties was a crucial element of freedom for former slaves.

travel freely. One preacher in northern Florida reminded his congregation of this new freedom:

> You aren't none o' you, going to feel really free till you shake the dust of the Old Plantation off your feet and go to a new place where you can live out off sight of the great house. . . . So long as the shadow of the great house falls across you, you aren't going to feel like a free man, and you aren't going to feel like a free woman. . . . You must all move—you must move clear away from the old places that you know, to the new places that you don't know, where you can raise up your head without any fear of Master This or Master Other. . . . Take your freedom, my brothers and my sisters. You-all are as good as anybody, and you-all are just as free! Go where you please—do what you please—forget about the white folks—and now stand up on your feet—lift up your eyes—and shout with me Glory, hallelujah! Amen!

Such sentiment was also expressed by a servant woman who, when offered a job by her former owner, said, "No, Miss, I must go. If I stay here I'll never know I am free."

Like the Florida preacher and the servant woman, Jourdon Anderson, a runaway slave during the Civil War, understood that freedom involved mobility and separating oneself from one's master. After Anderson escaped to Ohio in 1865, his former master requested his return to Tennessee, promising Anderson and his wife, Mandy, their freedom and compensation for their labor. Anderson's remarkable letter to his former owner explained his concept of emancipation, which included decent wages, proper respect, education for his children, and a place of worship of his choosing. Addressing his former master as an equal, Anderson described his new life in Ohio: "I get $25 a month, with victuals and clothing; have a comfortable home for Mandy (the folks here call her Mrs. Anderson) and the children, Milly, Jane and Grundy, go to school and are learning well."

Freed people characteristically defined freedom as the ability to make choices about how they would look and act. As one said, former

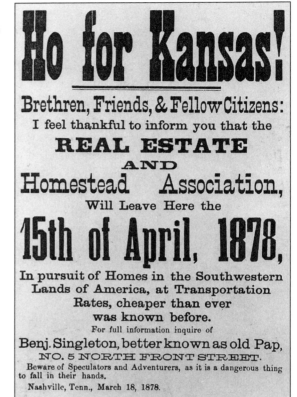

A poster tries to entice blacks to leave for the West. Many did leave the South in an attempt to start a new life.

slaves "wanted to make money like de white folks an' do deir own buyin'." They did not want to dress as they had during slavery, particularly on special occasions. Freed women typically bought new cloth for dresses to wear to church or on holidays because new clothes symbolized their new status. No longer slaves, they could chose their own apparel.

Freed people regarded the use of surnames as a sign of respect, as had Jourdon Anderson in Ohio. Whites had never called slaves by their surnames but demanded this courtesy from blacks. After the war, freed people began to choose their own last names. Even though some enslaved people had used last names, many had not. Sometimes freed people adopted the last name of their master at the time of the war or chose one of an earlier master. As one man explained, taking a master's surname "was done more because it was the logical thing to do and the easiest way to be identified than it was through affection for the master." This man chose, however, not to use his master's name. "I made up my mind I'd find me a different one. One of my grandfathers in Africa was called Jeaceo, and so I decided to be Jackson." When an army officer asked one soldier, "Do you want to be called by your old master's name?" he responded tersely, "No, sur, I don't. I'se had nuff o' ole massa." Sometimes freed people took names that they associated with their

On Christmas morning, a freedman and his family visit the home of his former master. Dressed in nice clothes for this social occasion, their gesture emphasizes the family's new status as the master's neighbors instead of his property.

emancipation, picking surnames like Freeman or Lincoln. One soldier's wife in Mississippi named her son General Grant.

Above all, freedom equaled autonomy, the ability to make decisions for oneself and in the best interests of one's family and community. Ultimately, it involved not having to take orders from a white master. As one former domestic slave, whose owner used to ring a bell when she wanted her, insisted, "answering bells is played out." African Americans also wanted to drop slavish mannerisms toward whites. They wanted the right to refuse to yield the right-of-way to whites when they met on the street or paths, to refuse to remove or tip their hats to white men who never reciprocated, and to be called by their surnames like an adult, not by their first names without a title, like a child. Grown African-American men resented being referred to as "boy" by whites. And freed people's expectations of freedom were interrelated: the ability to travel allowed both for slave families who had been separated to reunite and for those needing employment to move to new jobs.

Part of the quest for autonomy involved the desire of the freed people to own land and become economically independent rather than continue to work for whites. Francis L. Cardozo, an African-American

Black women sell sweet potatoes in Charleston, South Carolina. Choosing one's work was, for many, an essential part of freedom.

On the Sea Islands off the coast of South Carolina, freed slaves established farms and cultivated land, according to General Sherman's orders. Union officers even promised the land to those who worked it, but the transfer of land never occurred.

minister, educator, and politician, spoke in favor of land redistribution at the South Carolina constitutional convention after the Civil War. He argued that "in the North . . . every man has his own farm and is free and independent" and demanded, "Let the lands of the South be similarly divided. . . . We will never have true freedom until we abolish the system of agriculture which existed in the Southern States." Freed people argued that they deserved land because during slavery they had worked without compensation to make their owners wealthy. When asked by his former master to come work for him, Jourdon Anderson astutely suggested that his former master show good faith by giving Anderson and his wife "back pay" as slaves. "This will make us forget and forgive old scores, and rely on your justice and friendship in the future. I served you faithfully for thirty-two years and Mandy twenty years. At $25 a month for me, and $2 a week for Mandy, our earnings would amount to $11,680." Anderson even suggested that his former owner keep the interest on the unpaid money to pay for the clothing and medical care that Anderson and his family had received as slaves. Of course, Anderson did not really expect his former master to pay him back wages. Rather, he was pointing out the inequality of slavery as opposed to being a free person.

Freed people initially had reason to believe they would receive land from the federal government. In a few areas, the government divided up plantations deserted by slave owners who had escaped the Union soldiers. The government experimented with dividing land off the coast of South Carolina and at Davis

Senator Charles Sumner (right) and Representative Thaddeus Stevens were early advocates of civil rights. In Congress, they worked to enact legislation that would help former slaves secure fair treatment.

Bend, Mississippi. Davis Bend was part of the plantations of Confederate president Jefferson Davis and his brother Joseph. Some freed people did receive small plots, although the government sold or rented the vast majority of the land to white Northerners or Southerners loyal to the Union.

Concerned about the number of escaping slaves during the war, General William Tecumseh Sherman, on January 16, 1865, ordered parts of South Carolina near the coast and on the Sea Islands to be cultivated by freed slaves. According to Sherman's Special Order No. 15, the military would give each family 40 acres. Sherman also encouraged the army to lend the families army mules for plowing. He wanted freed families to become self-sufficient so that they would not depend on army supplies. In Georgia, freed people also established their own farms on land seized by the military. They worked hard to raise crops on these plots of land, did quite well, and also set up a limited local government in some areas. At the time, some military officers were so pleased by the results that they promised the land to the freed people, although such commitments were not honored after the war.

In March 1865, to encourage land ownership, Congress passed legislation stating that to "every male citizen, whether refugee or freedman, there shall be assigned not more than forty acres of land." However, this legislation was never put into effect because President Andrew Johnson vetoed the bill. In 1865, Johnson returned the plantations to the former owners once they promised loyalty to the U.S. government. Many years later, former slaves continued to express a sense of betrayal. More than 60 years after the war ended, Sally Dixon recalled, "We was told when we got freed we was going to get forty acres of land and a mule. 'Stead of that, we didn't get nothing."

Although the federal government did not give land to freed people, Congress did pass other laws to aid the former slaves. In the Senate, Charles Sumner of Massachusetts sponsored civil rights legislation and laws to aid the newly freed slaves, including provisions for having the federal government help establish schools. Before the Civil War, Sumner had been such a vocal critic of slavery and proslavery senators that he infuriated Representative Preston Brooks of South Carolina, who severely beat Sumner with a cane while he sat at his Senate desk. Sumner never fully recovered from the beating.

While Senator Sumner led the fight for freedmen's equity in the Senate, Thaddeus Stevens championed the cause of civil rights for African Americans in the House of Representatives. As a lawyer in Pennsylvania, Stevens had defended runaway slaves, arguing against their return. As a congressman, he bitterly opposed the Fugitive Slave Act that was passed as part of the Compromise of 1850. This act gave Southern whites the right to reenslave escaped slaves who had run away to the free states in the North. In spite of severe heart trouble, until his death in 1868 Stevens chaired the important Ways and Means Committee, which controls budgetary issues. With Sumner, Stevens was a member of the Joint Committee on Reconstruction that shaped Congressional Reconstruction policy regarding the South.

Under the leadership of men like Sumner and Stevens, the Republican-controlled Congress passed three amendments to the Constitution concerning the newly freed people. These changes were

Teacher Laura M. Towne with some of her pupils in Beaufort, South Carolina. The federal government supported efforts to educate former slaves, who would need literacy skills to compete for work and take control of their affairs.

accepted with the necessary two-thirds congressional majorities, after which three-fourths of the state legislatures voted for the amendments. They then became part of the Constitution. The 13th Amendment, abolishing slavery in the United States, was adopted by the states in 1865. The 14th Amendment, granting citizenship to freed people, was added to the Constitution in 1868. This right had been denied to slaves in an 1857 Supreme Court decision. The 15th Amendment guaranteed the right of African-American men—but not women—to vote. It was adopted in 1870. The 14th and 15th Amendments also allowed African-American men to vote for new state constitutions and state legislatures during the period known as Congressional Reconstruction, from roughly 1867 to 1869, when Congress implemented its plan for rebuilding the South. Congressional Reconstruction differed from Presidential Reconstruction, which had occurred from 1865 to 1867, by supporting the political rights of freedmen. During this era, African-American men ran for office, and won, while white Southern men who had supported the Confederacy were either temporarily disenfranchised or refused to vote, to protest the suffrage granted to African-American men.

Besides passing these three amendments, Congress overrode President Johnson's veto to establish the Bureau of Refugees, Freedmen, and Abandoned Lands, known as the Freedmen's Bureau. Its mission was to help freed people make the transition from slavery to freedom. The bureau gave out food to both Southern whites and African Americans if they needed it. It also provided an opportunity for former slaves to legalize their marriages, by issuing marriage licenses. Once the freed people realized they would not obtain land, bureau agents helped negotiate labor contracts between the freed people and their new employers and settle labor disputes. Establishing schools and hospitals was another part of the Freedmen's Bureau's work, particularly as it became clear that white Southerners wanted facilities that excluded African Americans.

Understaffed and underfunded, the Freedmen's Bureau did not always work the way Congress intended. Sometimes its employees living in the South were overly sympathetic to white employers and prejudiced against African Americans. Also, freed people found it hard to take time off from work to walk to the bureau in the closest town and make a claim against an employer.

Besides passing legislation to set up the Freedmen's Bureau, Congress tried to protect freed people's rights through other laws. Congress

Black residents of New York City celebrate the adoption of the 15th Amendment, which guaranteed the right of African-American males to vote. Women, both black and white, could not vote until the 19th Amendment was ratified in 1920.

passed the Civil Rights Act of 1866 to overturn the discriminatory Black Codes that Southern states had passed after 1865 to limit the rights of African Americans. Although President Johnson demanded that the Southern states abolish slavery by ratifying the 13th Amendment, he encouraged Southern state legislatures to reject the concepts of African-American suffrage and equality.

Immediately after the Civil War, during what is referred to as Presidential Reconstruction, Southern state legislatures under the control of whites sympathetic to the Confederacy passed laws that applied only to African Americans. These laws, passed from 1865 to 1866, attempted to thwart African Americans' visions of freedom and their quest for individual and community independence. These Black Codes bestowed certain legal rights on former slaves, such as the right to enter into contracts legally. As a result, freed people gained the right to marry and acquire personal property.

More significantly, however, the Black Codes limited various aspects of African Americans' lives. Most states passed vagrancy laws, which meant that African Americans had to prove they were employed by whites or risk arrest. To further ensure that African Americans were available for employment by whites, the states passed strict rules enforcing year-long labor contracts so that workers could not change employers for at least a full year, even for higher wages. In Florida, employees who broke their contracts could suffer physical punishment or be required to provide a full year's labor without pay. Mississippi passed some of the most repressive laws, such as legislation prohibiting African Americans from possessing guns and leasing or renting land in rural areas. Some Black Codes also allowed former masters or other whites to apprentice or have the children of former slaves work for them if the courts ruled that the children's parents were destitute. Thus, former slave owners could keep African-American boys until they reached 21 and girls until they turned 18 without paying them or their parents anything for their labor. The Black Codes also forbade interracial marriage and prohibited African Americans from serving on juries. Although the Black Codes allowed African Americans to be witnesses in court, they could not testify against a white person.

Along with the passage of the Black Codes, white vigilante groups sprang up throughout the South to terrorize African Americans and keep them from exercising their vision as free people. The best-known such organization was the Ku Klux Klan, which was formed in Tennessee in 1866. An early leader of the Klan was Nathan Bedford Forrest, a Confederate soldier and former slave owner whose men were responsible for butchering African-American men at Fort Pillow, Tennessee, during the Civil War. The Klan and other groups targeted whites and African-American men and their families who were active in the Republican party as well as white and African-American schoolteachers. They also attacked black landowners and those refusing to behave in a manner subservient to whites.

Through their dealings with Southern whites, African Americans learned that freedom could not be easily attained but would involve

Members of the Mississippi Ku Klux Klan in their outfits, which hid their identities as they terrorized blacks in an attempt to keep them submissive to whites.

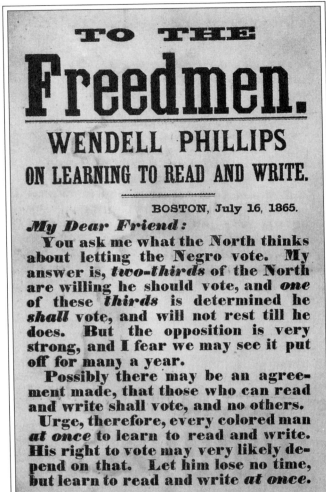

TO THE
Freedmen.
WENDELL PHILLIPS
ON LEARNING TO READ AND WRITE.

BOSTON, July 16, 1865.

My Dear Friend:

You ask me what the North thinks about letting the Negro vote. My answer is, *two-thirds* of the North are willing he should vote, and *one* of these *thirds* is determined he *shall* vote, and will not rest till he does. But the opposition is very strong, and I fear we may see it put off for many a year.

Possibly there may be an agreement made, that those who can read and write shall vote, and no others.

Urge, therefore, every colored man *at once* to learn to read and write. His right to vote may very likely depend on that. Let him lose no time, but learn to read and write *at once*.

Yours truly,

Mr. JAMES REDPATH.   WENDELL PHILLIPS.

This public letter from reformer Wendell Phillips urges blacks to educate themselves so they can assume the duties of citizenship.

struggle. Freed people adopted a variety of methods to try to ensure what they considered freedom. When possible, they made complaints to the Freedmen's Bureau regarding white injustices. On plantations they joined together to demand better wages and working conditions. Within their communities they established their own churches and schools. With the passage of the 14th Amendment to the Constitution, African-American men, along with women and children, marched to polling places. There, the men cast their votes for Republican candidates to help ensure civil rights for themselves and their communities.

There can be no doubt that slave men and women wanted their freedom. One Union soldier had the following discussion with a slave man who had run away to the Union lines:

"How were you treated, Robert?

"Pretty well, sir."

"Did your master give you enough to eat and clothe you comfortably?"

"Pretty well, till dis year. Massa hab no money to spend dis year. Don't get many clothes dis year."

"If you had a good master, I suppose you were contented?"

"No, sir."

"Why not, if you had enough to eat and clothes to wear?"

"Cause I want to be free."

MEMBERS OF THE LEGISLATURE
OF THE
STATE OF MISSISSIPPI, 1874-'75.
PHOTOGRAPHED BY **E. von SEUTTER**, JACKSON, MISS.

A—SENATE.

1 Lt.-Gov A. K. Davis, Pres
2 W. C. White, Secretary.
3 Little, Finis H.
4 Warner, Alex.
5 Campbell, M.
6 McClure, H. B.
7 Carter, J. P.
8 Thornton, P. R.
9 Mendenhall, J. L.
10 Sessions J. F.
11 Metis, M. A.
12 Tuttle M. H.
13 Taylor, R. H.
14 Furlong, C. E.
15 Graham, T. B.
16 Price, W. M.
17 Stone, J. M.
18 Allen, R H.
19 Everett, J. E.
20 Bridges, N. B.
21 McNeil, J. A.
22 Cullens, C.
23 Bennett, Jos.
24 Steel, S. A D.
25 Gillmer, J. P.
26 Henderson,
27 Gray, Will.
28 Barrow, P. B.
29 White, G. W.
30 Smith, G. C.
31 Stuart Isham
32 Gleed, Rob.
33 Williams, J. M. P.
34 Caldwell, Chas.
35 Albright, G W
36 Miss Adie Ball, Post M.

B—HOUSE DEMOCRATS.

1 Street, H M
2 Leggott, S
3 Crecelius, J G
4 Green, H C
5 Archer, B F
6 Gilmer, W B
7 Cooke, H A
8 Byrd, C
9 Byrd, R
10 Smith, John T
11 Spight, Thos
12 Stockstill, Thos
13 Stubbs, G W
14 Demson, J N
15 Eckford, J M.
16 Rogers, D W
17 Martin, J
18 Thames W H
19 Walker, J M
20 Graham, D A
21 Ackers, Jack.
22 Applewhite, R R
23 Horton, H C
24 Boyd, J M
25 Horton, G G
26 Garrett, T B
27 Reese, J L
28 Campbell, C H
29 Tison, W H H
30 Champlin, W A
31 Atkins, T C
32 Gilmer, W B
33 Thompson, J P
34 Chandler, J W
35 Wynn, B L
36 Devall, E M
37 Thompson, W W
38 Southworth H H.

*Republican.

C—HOUSE REPUBLICANS.

1 Shadd, J. D. Spenker
2 Warren, H W Ch. Clerk
3 Sullivan, M B
4 Feemster, R M D
5 Ford, O C
6 Baffkin, D
7 Stephens, Z M
8 Foxworth, J P
9 Stone J M
10 Gill, N G
11 Gill, N G
12 Palmer, B
13 Chamberlin A M
14 Clover, F A
15 Hasle, Geo
16 Makey, L W
17 Shalttick
18 Cowart, E O
19 Richards,
20 Peyton, E A
21 Willburn, E B
22 Boyd, Octi
23 Smothers, J
24 Harrison, H H
25 Chrismas, R
26 Chiles, Benj.
27 Monroe, J E
28 Williams, R
29 Washington, G
30 Edwards, W W
31 Kendrick, R
32 Shirley, (Senate) †
33 Boyd, of Yazoo
34 Caradine, J W
35 Lynch, W H
36 Landers, W R
37 Cessor, J D
38 Peal, A
39 Truehart, H H
40 Brunt, O
41 Morgan, J H
42 McFarland, J W
43 Weatherly, T
44 Davis, Willis
45 White, G W
46 Cotton, T A
47 Hundy, A.
48 Harris, W. H.
49 Moseley, G. G.
50 Jones, W. H.
51 Richards, E. A.
52 Mathews, D. T. J.
53 Rogers, A. A.
54 McCain, Thos.
55 Patterson, J. G.
56 Randolph. J. W.
57 Gayles. G. W.
58 Sykes, T.
59 Clemons. C. P.
60 Simmons, J. S.
61 Boyd, of Warren.
62 Chavis, Wash.
63 Walker, J. C.
64 Fitzhugh, S. W.
65 Green, D. S.
66 Smith, of Tunica,
67 McNeese, M.
68 Nathan, Cato.
69 Hicks, Wilson
70 Johnson, J. H.
71 Smith, H.
72 Thompson, R.
73 Howard, P.
74 Trotter, Ast. Serg.-Arms.
75 Pease, Sergt-at-Arms.

† Senator

Politics: "Slavery Is Not Abolished Until the Black Man Has the Ballot"

◇ ◇ ◇

As a young child, Robert Smalls was a well-treated house servant. When he was 12, his master hired him out as an urban slave. He worked on the docks at Charleston, South Carolina, and learned sailmaking. Then in May, 1862, in his 20s, Smalls and his wife, Hannah, decided to escape slavery by stealing a Confederate boat and sailing it to freedom. The one they took was a boat Smalls worked on, which had a slave crew and three white officers. There were 16 people, including Smalls's family, on the ship early one morning while the white crew members were still sleeping onshore. With a straw hat hiding his face, Smalls guided the boat past the Confederate posts, correctly signaling the Confederate codes. Some Confederates thought the boat was out patroling very early, but they allowed it through the checkpoints. After passing the last point, Smalls dropped the Confederate flag and raised a white bed sheet as a sign of truce. Then he sailed to Charleston, which the Union forces controlled, and turned over the boat to the Union soldiers. Smalls not only won his freedom but the U.S. Congress paid him a reward for providing the Union army with a working Confederate war vessel.

Robert Smalls went on to serve as a second lieutenant in the Union navy. In 1864, while waiting for his boat to be repaired in Philadelphia, he was thrown off a streetcar. The protests that resulted from this incident led the streetcar companies to integrate their cars. After the war,

The Mississippi legislature of 1874–75 includes several black representatives. At the time, Mississippi had more African-American officeholders than most other states.

These men served in the Virginia General Assembly in 1887–88. During Reconstruction, blacks were able for the first time to vote for the office-holders who would best represent their interests.

Smalls continued his political activism. As he grew more successful, Smalls compensated as a free adult for his lack of formal education during slavery. From five to seven o'clock each morning, he studied on his own and, for the next two hours, had private lessons. To improve his reading ability, he subscribed to a newspaper. He became a delegate to the South Carolina constitutional convention. In 1870, he won a seat in the South Carolina senate and served as a U.S. congressman. Smalls became one of the most influential politicians in South Carolina during Reconstruction, supporting public education and voting rights for African-American men.

During Reconstruction, for the first time, African Americans in the South held office in local and state governments and even became lawmakers in the U.S. Congress. Some of these lawmakers had been free before the war, but others, like Smalls, were formerly enslaved. Guaranteeing and protecting the right of African-American male suffrage was important to these leaders, as it was to Smalls. In the face of intense— even violent—opposition, they served in public office.

Before the end of the Civil War, African Americans participated in meetings, organizations, and conventions to voice their political concerns and aspirations. In 1864, African Americans met in Syracuse, New York, to form the National Equal Rights League. The league encouraged states to form branches. African Americans in New Orleans formed their own chapter. Calling for African-American male suffrage, the league championed other civil rights issues and demanded, for example, that African Americans be permitted to sit wherever they wanted on streetcars rather than being relegated to the dirtiest, most crowded cars or having to stay on the platform outside.

During Reconstruction, African Americans throughout the country participated in civil rights groups called Union Leagues. Many of the leagues were racially segregated, but some included both African American and white Republicans, working together to oppose the former Confederates, who were Democrats. Union Leagues often supported reforms on the local level such as protesting all-white juries and raising money to build schools and churches. Committed to the issue of workers' rights, the leagues provided advice on negotiating for better wages and even organized strikes in Alabama and South Carolina. To keep mobs of whites from interrupting their meetings, the league often encouraged African-American men to arm themselves when attending. On some of these occasions, black women kept guard over stacks of weapons.

The jury selected to hear the trial of Jefferson Davis (who was indicted for treason) included several black men.

During and after the war, African Americans organized state conventions to advance the political and economic issues of significance to them. These conventions demanded such rights as being allowed to serve on a jury, gain an education, and carry guns. "We claim exactly the same rights, privileges and immunities as are enjoyed by white men—we ask nothing more and will be content with nothing less," declared a statement from the 1865 Alabama convention. It continued: "The law no longer knows white nor black, but simply men, and consequently we are entitled to ride in public conveyances, hold office, sit on juries and do everything else which we have in the past been prevented from doing solely on the ground of color." At the South Carolina convention, William B. Nash, who later became a state senator, summed up several of these demands: "We ask that the three great agents of civilized society—the school, the pulpit, the press—be as secure in South Carolina as in Massachusetts, or in Vermont. We ask that equal suffrage be conferred upon us, in common with the white men of this state." At first it was the African Americans who had been free before the war who controlled the convention agendas, but increasingly freedmen became active.

Immediately after the war, Southern and Northern blacks began to agitate for voting privileges for African-American men. Frederick Douglass, a former slave and an abolitionist, argued that "slavery is not abolished until the black man has the ballot." African-American men petitioned the government to grant them the right to vote, arguing that "if we are called on to do military duty against the rebel armies in the field, why should we be denied the privilege of voting against rebel citizens at the ballot-box?"

Tying the vote to military service automatically excluded African-American women from being considered for suffrage. Neither political party endorsed woman suffrage, and the issue lost in several state referenda across the country. Failure to receive the vote did not keep African-American women from other kinds of political activity, however, such as declaring their loyalty to the Republican party through wearing campaign buttons, attending meetings, and marching with their men to the voting places.

President Lincoln favored limited African-American male suffrage, for "the very intelligent, and [for] those who serve our cause as soldiers," but he did not make the advocacy of black male suffrage part of his plan for the South. When he became confident that the North would win the

This 1881 lithograph, entitled Heroes of the Colored Race, *shows Frederick Douglass (middle) with Blanche K. Bruce (left) and Hiram Revels (right), both U.S. senators from Mississippi.*

Civil War, he began to work out measures to deal with the Southern states involved in the rebellion. Under Lincoln's policy, men highly placed in the Confederate army or government would not immediately regain their right to vote, but most Southern men would not be punished if they promised to support the U.S. government and accept the end of slavery. Lincoln's plan allowed that after 10 percent of a state's 1860 voting population declared its loyalty to the Union, the state could establish a new government. Only three Confederate states agreed to Lincoln's policy: Louisiana, Arkansas, and Tennessee. Because Lincoln developed this plan during the war, it remains unclear how he would have dealt with the South once the war ended.

Members of Congress reviewing Lincoln's plan felt it was too conciliatory to Confederates and did not go far enough in protecting the newly freed slaves. Congress exercised its prerogative not to allow representatives from Louisiana, Arkansas, or Tennessee to join the U.S.

Congress. Additionally, Congress countered Lincoln's policies with the Wade-Davis Bill, which temporarily placed the former Confederate states under military control. Rather than automatically having these states represented in Congress, as in Lincoln's plan, this bill had the President appoint governors to oversee the transition within the former Confederate states. Under these governors, a majority of the voting population (as opposed to Lincoln's 10 percent) had to swear loyalty, after which each state was required to pass a new state constitution outlawing slavery. Like Lincoln's plan, in this one high-ranking Confederate government and military men could not vote. In addition, only men who swore that they had not supported the Confederacy or fought against the Union could vote for delegates to write the new state constitutions. This test of loyalty was referred to as the "ironclad oath." The Wade-Davis Bill also provided freed people with limited civil rights. Because Lincoln refused to sign the Wade-Davis bill, it never became law.

Lincoln and Congress were never able to work out a compromise for reconstructing the South. On April 14, 1865, while enjoying a play with his wife at Ford's Theatre, in Washington, a proslavery actor named John Wilkes Booth shot the President in the head with a pistol. Booth himself fell onstage, breaking his left leg. Some members of the audience thought he yelled in Latin, "Thus be it ever to tyrants." Booth limped outside and rode away. Early the next day, President Lincoln died. On April 26, apparently, a soldier who was trying to capture Booth shot and killed him.

Upon Lincoln's death, Vice President Andrew Johnson assumed the Presidency. Johnson, a former slave owner, had remained loyal to the Union. He was a compromise candidate for Vice President, chosen to appease the border states and slave owners not in rebellion. Johnson's plan for Reconstruction, referred to as Presidential Reconstruction, was in effect from 1865 until 1867. It differed from Congress's later plan, referred to as Congressional Reconstruction. Johnson's proposals included making white Southerners from Confederate states take loyalty oaths to the Union and called for the writing of new Southern state constitutions. They specified the election of new state governments before a state's representatives to the U.S. Congress would be accepted. Johnson demanded that Southern whites owning more than $20,000 worth of property request a special Presidential pardon as a way of further humiliating them.

When Lincoln was assassinated, his plans for Reconstruction, which were somewhat conciliatory toward the South, were abandoned. At right is the sheet music cover of a march composed to mark the President's death.

Unlike many members of Congress, Johnson showed little concern over the status of freed people, believing that they needed to be controlled by Southern whites. After presenting his plan for Reconstruction, Johnson vetoed a bill funding the Freedmen's Bureau and the Civil Rights Act of 1866. However, Congress obtained the two-thirds majority required to override a veto, and both bills became law. Johnson tried to undercut Congress's position by attempting to sabotage its efforts at Reconstruction of the South. The ongoing disagreements between Johnson and Congress over governmental policies regarding Reconstruction caused a widening rift between the executive and legislative branches of government. Congress passed a law that the President could not remove Presidential appointments approved by the Senate, but Johnson ignored it. Hostilities grew to the point where the Congress actually impeached the President, although in 1868 it voted not to remove him from office.

As President, Andrew Johnson confronted a hostile Congress that disagreed with him about the best way to rebuild the South. In 1868, Johnson was impeached by the House of Representatives, but the Senate acquitted him and he was not removed from office.

The Southern states were quick to accept many facets of Johnson's plan for Reconstruction because much of it was more agreeable to them than Congress's. In 1865–66, white men—many of whom were former Confederates and slave owners—were elected as delegates to rewrite the state constitutions and soon after became state legislators. Although the states' revised constitutions recognized the end of slavery, the state legislatures in most Southern states also passed the Black Codes, which restricted African Americans' civil rights.

Angered in part by the Black Codes, by white attacks against African Americans in race riots in Memphis and New Orleans in May and July 1866, and by the Southern states' unwillingness to accept civil rights for newly freed slaves, the U.S. Congress decided that a plan tougher than Johnson's was needed. For one thing, Congress refused to accept senators and representatives elected from the states that had adopted Johnson's Reconstruction plan. Then, in 1866, Congress passed the 14th Amendment to the U.S. Constitution, which granted citizenship to African Americans and ensured that they were counted in the population for representation purposes in the House of Representatives.

In 1866, whites attacked African Americans in Memphis, resulting in a race riot. Such episodes of violence helped persuade Congress to pass legislation that would ensure the rights of black citizens.

Congress further declared that any man who had supported the Confederacy could not be elected to any state or federal office unless Congress approved. This provision incidentally helped promote the Republican party in the South because most of the men disenfranchised were Democrats. Although accepting the 14th Amendment was a prerequisite for congressional recognition of a state's representatives and senators, all the Southern state legislatures except Tennessee initially voted against the 14th Amendment. It ultimately passed in 1868.

In 1867, Congress acted on its own Reconstruction plan. Congress placed military commanders with federal troops in charge of the former Confederate states. Although the Southern states complained about having Union troops stationed in the South, by the end of 1866 only 38,000 remained, mostly in frontier areas.

Another part of Congressional Reconstruction was its requirement that the former Confederate states rewrite their constitutions to supersede those passed during Presidential Reconstruction. A state could then set up a state legislature and, if it ratified the 14th Amendment, be readmitted into the Union and have its representatives accepted in the U.S. Congress. To guarantee African-American men the right to vote, Con-

This print (left) commemorating the revision of Louisiana's state constitution includes portraits of African-American figures who participated in the process. During Presidential Reconstruction, Confederate states had to rewrite their constitutions to recognize the end of slavery.

gress also passed the 15th Amendment to the United States Constitution. It was ratified by the states in 1870.

The new state constitutions written during Congressional Reconstruction were often the most democratic ones passed in the South. They provided funds for public schools, railroad construction, and other improvements needed in part because of war damage. They supported services for the poor and physically disabled as well as the establishment of orphan asylums. The state constitutions also included such progressive measures as abolishing imprisonment for owing money and public whippings as punishment for crimes. Through the revised constitutions and new state laws, much of the racially discriminatory legislation passed under the Black Codes was eliminated.

The Republican-dominated Congress supported African-American male suffrage, in part because some members believed that blacks would achieve equity and justice only if they received suffrage. Congress also knew that freed people would be more likely to vote for the Republican rather than the Democratic party. African Americans supported the Republican party because Republicans endorsed equal rights and the end of slavery, whereas the Democrats had opposed the federal government's ending of slavery.

Congressional Reconstruction made available unprecedented political opportunities for African-American men in the South. Even Northern African Americans headed South to become community leaders and officeholders. On the local level, African Americans became increasingly active, electing men to positions as mayors, police chiefs, school commissioners, and state militia officers. They sat on juries and became policemen and tax collectors. Nineteen African Americans in Louisiana and 15 in Mississippi became sheriffs. African-American coroners as well as racially integrated juries and sheriffs helped African Americans receive the justice denied to them as slaves. Local black leaders built coalitions with other African Americans to help influence state policies and aid in electing African Americans to offices at the state level.

African Americans voted in large numbers for state delegates to the new state constitutional conventions at a time when many white Democrats who had supported the Confederacy were refusing to vote. With these elections, African Americans became part of the constitutional delegations in the South. Whites, including both Northern Republicans who had moved to the South as well as Southern whites who had stayed

FROM THE PLANTATION TO THE SENATE.

This poster pays tribute to senators who were once slaves; their portraits flank that of Frederick Douglass. Although he never held elected office, Douglass did serve as a U.S. marshal for the District of Columbia and as U.S. minister to Haiti.

loyal to the Union during the war, made up the majority of the delegates. Only in Louisiana and South Carolina were African Americans the majority in the delegations.

When state elections were held after the ratification of the new state constitutions, male voters of both races overwhelmingly elected

Republicans, both white and African-American. Many black delegates to the state constitutional conventions later became state legislators. African Americans representatives advocated land redistribution, equal access to public schools, women's rights, a 10-hour workday rather than having laborers work from sunup to sundown, and prohibitions against family violence. They also argued for racially integrated restaurants, hotels, theaters, and transportation systems. Although African-American legislators disagreed among themselves on many of these issues, almost all wanted full political rights for African Americans.

Besides serving at the state and local levels, African Americans were also elected to national office. Sixteen African-American men served in the U.S. Congress during Reconstruction. In 1870, Hiram Revels from Mississippi became the first African-American U.S. senator. He took the Senate seat once held by Jefferson Davis, who had resigned to become President of the Confederacy. Before the war, Revels's parents, as free blacks, had lived in North Carolina. Revels attended college, became a minister at the African Methodist Episcopal Church in Baltimore, and was a chaplain for an African-American regiment stationed in Vicksburg, Mississippi. Revels also recruited black soldiers for the Union army.

Joseph Rainey of South Carolina served for four terms in the U.S. Congress.

Blanche Kelso Bruce also served as a U.S. senator. As a slave in Missouri, Bruce had become a printer. During the war, he ran a school for African-American children. Then he went to Mississippi, where he became a sheriff and a tax collector. After election to the Senate, he worked on such issues as Indian policy, improvements to the Mississippi River, and racial equity.

Joseph H. Rainey of South Carolina was the first African American to serve in the U.S. House of Representatives. Rainey had been a free African American before the Civil War and had worked in Charleston, South Carolina. Robert P. Elliot was a delegate to the South Carolina constitutional convention and served in the South Carolina House of Repre-

sentatives, becoming speaker in 1874–76. He was also a U.S. congressman. In Alabama, three African Americans served as congressmen including James T. Rapier. Rapier supported expanding public funds for education rather than relying solely on private schools, and he helped freed people obtain land in the West.

Alonzo J. Ransier, born in England, was another South Carolina congressman. Free before the war, he worked as a clerk for a shipping office. John R. Lynch, the son of a slave woman and a white man, became free during the Civil War. After serving as justice of the peace, he was elected as a representative to the Mississippi legislature and served two terms in the U.S. House of Representatives. He advocated voting rights for African-American men.

Robert Elliot (left) addresses his fellow representatives in this 1874 lithograph entitled The Shackle Broken—By the Genius of Freedom.

Pinckney B. S. Pinchback, governor of Louisiana during Reconstruction, was the only black governor in the nation. Whites still held most of the high offices at the state and national levels.

In the South during Reconstruction, most of the highest state offices were held by whites. Only Louisiana had an African-American governor, Pinckney B. S. Pinchback. He supported African-American male suffrage, education for freed people, and integrated accommodations on trains and boats. Mississippi and South Carolina both had African-American lieutenant governors. In Louisiana and South Carolina, African Americans served as state treasurers. African Americans became secretary of state in Florida, Mississippi, and South Carolina. Arkansas, Florida, Louisiana, and Mississippi had African-American superintendents of education during Reconstruction. In some states, these officials oversaw the development of the first state public school systems for whites as well as blacks.

The African-American lawmakers serving at the state level came from a variety of backgrounds. Some, like James Lynch of Mississippi, were free Northern African Americans before Reconstruction. Educated in Pennsylvania, he went to Mississippi after the war to work for the Methodist Episcopal Church. During the war, Lynch served as a cook in the army. As he wrote in his diary, "I have convictions of duty to my race as deep as my own soul. . . . They impel me to go [to] a Southern state, and unite my destiny with that of my people." Lynch campaigned for the Republican party, organized a Loyal League to support it, and became secretary of state in Mississippi. On July 4, 1865, speaking to freed people in Augusta, Georgia, Lynch argued that "all that my race asks of the white man is justice." Francis L. Cardozo worked as a carpenter, saved his earnings, and went to Europe for an education. A minister, he traveled in the South to train African-American teachers. Cardozo, a delegate to the South Carolina state constitutional convention, later became the first African-American secretary of state.

More than 600 African-American men were elected to state legislatures in the South, although whites continued to chair most of the important committees. Except in Louisiana and South Carolina, most of the black legislators were former slaves. South Carolina legislator Will-

iam R. Jervey had escaped slavery and served in the Union army. And Prince Rivers, also in the South Carolina legislature, had driven his white owner's coach. During the war, he stole his master's horse and fled to the Union lines, where he became a soldier. His white officer praised him: "There is not a white officer in this regiment who has more administrative ability or more absolute authority over the men; they do not love him, but his mere presence has controlling power over them . . . and if there should ever be a black monarchy in South Carolina, he will be its king." A successful farmer and contractor, Rivers served as a trial justice before becoming a magistrate.

During Reconstruction, resistance was fierce to African-American lawmakers and Northern-born as well as Southern white Republicans who dominated Southern legislatures. Whites formed secret organizations such as the Ku Klux Klan and White Camelia. Well-armed groups

An 1871 engraving shows Klan members in North Carolina about to murder a black man. Such organized white violence was committed in an attempt to keep blacks from gaining political power, which threatened white dominance.

like the Red Shirts, rifle clubs, and white leagues like the Klan tried to keep African-American men from voting and killed or drove out African-American politicians from their homes, even sometimes out of the South. As historian Eric Foner has explained, "In effect, the Klan was a military force serving the interest of the Democratic party, the planter class, and all those who desired the restoration of white supremacy." One freedman recalled that Klansmen assaulted African Americans and once "ravished a young girl who was visiting my wife." He explained, "The cause of this treatment, they said, was that we voted the radical [Republican] ticket."

Ku Klux Klan violence devastated the Loyal League and made holding mass political meetings increasingly difficult for African Americans. One African-American minister recalled being terrorized by the Klan: "The republican paper was then coming to me from Charleston. It came to my name. They said I must stop it, quit preaching, and put a card in the newspaper renouncing republicanism, and they would not kill me; but if I did not they would come back the next week and kill me." In his testimony to Congress, one African-American justice of the peace in Tennessee stated that Klansmen assaulted him "because I had the impudence to run against a white man for office, and beat him." An attempted murder of an African-American politician in Alabama was justified by whites, according to testimony about Klan activities, on the grounds that he "was going around instructing and enlightening negroes how to act and how to work for their rights, and to make contracts to get their rights." The Klan sent a message to a black Georgia congressman expressing its contempt: "For we swear by the powers of both *Light and Darkness* that no Negro shall enter the Legislative Halls of the South." Even faced with such opposition, African Americans continued to serve at the national, state, and local levels. Georgia state senator Aaron Bradley, along with other African Americans, fought against the Klan. He wrote a public notice to the "KKK and all Bad Men" that stated, "If you strike a blow the man or men will be followed, and house in which he or they shall take shelter, will be burned to the ground."

African Americans resisted white vigilantism, but they could not fight the combined legal and illegal methods whites used to disenfranchise black voters. In Alabama, African Americans told Klansmen that "they were willing to go out into an open field and 'fight it out.'" But such courageous stands could not effectively protect white and African-American Republicans. Resistance to the Klan and other white violence was dangerous because local whites often did not support African Americans' attempts to retaliate against the Klan. Also, the Klan often possessed superior weapons. African Americans correctly feared that armed confrontation with Klan members and other white vigilantes would increase the likelihood that whites would retaliate and spread the violence against African Americans. During 1870 and 1871, the United States passed Enforcement Acts, which expanded the use of federal courts against election fraud, and in 1871, the Ku Klux Klan Act gave the federal government the right to use federal courts as well as troops against groups conspiring to keep people from voting, sitting on juries, or holding public office. When troops were used in South Carolina, violence declined for a short time in the South.

Whites did not have to be part of the KKK to intimidate and attack blacks, as this 1875 cartoon reveals. Here, a federal officer—one of many stationed throughout the South after the war—intervenes.

Nonviolent means were also used to keep African Americans from participating in government. In Georgia in 1868, the state legislature refused to allow duly elected African-American members to attend state congressional sessions, on the grounds that because of their race, the African Americans did not possess the right to serve as lawmakers. The black legislators were finally seated by order of the U.S. Congress. Many white Republicans involved in political coalitions with African Americans preferred that the blacks not hold office but simply elect white Republicans to represent them. The majority of Southern whites never fully accepted the idea of African-American male suffrage, and many secretly hoped to subvert it once the federal government removed its troops from the region.

After a lull during the election of 1872 because of federal intervention, violence flared again. In Mississippi, an African-American sheriff pleaded in a letter to the governor for federal troops to protect African-American officeholders and voters. He observed, "A perfect state of terror reigns supreme throughout the county." During the election of 1875, when violent white mobs tried to keep African-American men from voting, one black policeman told his former master, "We are gwine to have this election; we mean to get it by fair means if we can, but we are bound to have it anyhow." Besides violence aimed at keeping African-American men from voting, Southern whites also refused to rent them land or give them credit or jobs if they supported the Republican party. As one African-American lawmaker recalled, "I always had plenty of work before I went into politics, but I never got a job since." He conjectured that whites refused to hire him "because they think they will break me down and keep [me] from interfering with politics."

During the 1870s, Northern commitment to Reconstruction began to wane. Republicans split over issues such as corruption, tariffs, and free trade. Corruption in government, including bribery of officials, was a problem nationwide after the war. Economic growth and particularly the expansion of the railroads were accompanied by attempts to sway politicians, whether by lawful or unlawful methods. While corruption and graft were much greater in the North than the South, Reconstruction was often blamed for the dishonesty in government. It was the white Southern politicians who received much more in illegal payments and railroad stocks than the African-American lawmakers, but some black lawmakers were also found to have accepted bribes. Railroad companies handed out money or stock to gain state legislators' support for their projects, inducing politicians to vote for projects in which they had an economic interest. U.S. Congressman Robert Smalls of South Carolina, along with others, was convicted of taking a bribe, although he was later pardoned.

In the North, whites wearied of the turmoil of Reconstruction. Many began to believe that peace would occur only if the Southern whites, particularly the planters, controlled Southern state governments and African Americans, even though this meant that white domination would subvert the ideal of equal rights. After 1872, the federal government became increasingly unwilling to use federal troops to stop violence against African-American voters and lawmakers. In that same year, Congress gave back the right to vote to most Confederate supporters. As a result of whites voting once more, the desertion of some Southern whites from the Republican party, and the disenfranchisement of some African-American male voters through violence and other means, more Democrats were elected and took control of state governments in the South. As one African-American politician noted, "The whole South—every state in the South—had got into the hands of the very men that held us as slaves." These men favored a white supremacist government and society, with African Americans subservient to whites in their political, economic, and social relationships. These white legislators enacted various methods of keeping blacks from voting. Along with moving polling places into white areas and providing fewer ones where African Americans lived, they also passed poll taxes and established property qualifications for voting. Poor African Americans who could not afford to pay the poll tax could not vote. As a result, fewer African American lawmakers were elected. White officials also increasingly barred blacks from serving on juries.

In 1876, the federal government withdrew even its marginal support for Reconstruction. In the Presidential election of that year, the Democratic candidate, Samuel J. Tilden, won the popular vote over the Republican nominee, Rutherford B. Hayes. Because in some states, particularly in the South, the votes were contested with both parties declaring victory, Tilden did not gain the needed electoral college votes. In 1877 Congress worked out a compromise through a special election commission that decided in favor of Hayes by one vote. Meanwhile, Republican and Democratic leaders informally decided that if Southern congressmen would accept Hayes, he would withdraw federal troops

In one instance of government corruption, leading members of the House and Senate as well as the Vice President accepted stock in the Credit Mobilier company in return for passing legislation favorable to a railroad construction project.

Federal troops file out of Louisiana in accordance with an order from President Rutherford B. Hayes. When the troops left Louisiana and South Carolina, Reconstruction was officially over.

from the South. Such a policy, which Hayes had favored even before the election, would allow white Southerners to disenfranchise Southern black men without federal interference. Southern Democrats also wanted more control over federal jobs in the South and federal help in financing road construction, bridge repair, and other such improvements.

The African-American men who held office during Reconstruction provided Southern blacks with more legal equity than they had previously received as slaves or would gain under legislatures controlled by the Democrats after Reconstruction. The new constitutions passed during Reconstruction instituted many reforms within the South. The political failure of Reconstruction, during and after the Reconstruction era, was that these achievements were often undermined.

CHAPTER 4

LABOR: "I MEAN TO OWN MY OWN MANHOOD"

◇ ◇ ◇

Major Martin Delaney, one of the few African Americans to become an officer in the U.S. Army during the Civil War, went to South Carolina as a Freedmen's Bureau agent in 1865. He delivered a speech encouraging freed people to refuse to accept poor working conditions. First he reminded them of the wealth produced by slaves: "People say that you are too lazy to work, that you have not the intelligence to get on yourselves. . . . You men and women, every one of you around me, made thousands and thousands of dollars. Only you were the means for your master to lead the idle and inglorious life, and to give his children the education which he denied to you for fear you may awake to conscience." Then Delaney denounced the inequity of free (non-slave) labor: "Now I look around me and I notice a man, bare footed covered with rags and dirt. Now I ask, what is that man doing, for whom is he working. I hear that he worked for 30 cents a day. I tell you that must not be. That would be cursed slavery over again." Delaney's speech raised significant issues for freed people such as low wages and the failure of African Americans to receive just compensation for their servitude. He also stressed that even with freedom, few blacks were reaching the degree of economic independence from whites that they desired.

Black longshoremen on the banks of the James River in Virginia. Mostly freed slaves, these men hoped to find work that would grant them economic independence from whites.

Most blacks failed to achieve the level of economic well-being that Major Delaney and the freed people hoped for immediately after the war. During Reconstruction, a small minority of African Americans became landowners with small family farms. In South Carolina, for instance, the state government helped some gain small homesteads. But those who became landowners were the exception. By the end of Reconstruction, most African Americans in the South still worked at agricultural labor for white employers, doing the same kind of work they had done as slaves—but now they expected to be paid for it.

Freed people expected free labor, in contrast to slavery, to mean fewer work hours and more control over their work. Freedom meant no more overseers, no more beatings. Workers now expected to be able to leave their employers at will, for better wages or improved working conditions. The former slave masters, however, often disagreed with this definition of free labor. They expected their laborers to go on working from sunup to sundown as before, with one payment at the end of the year, and under many of the same restrictions as under slavery. The

Many freed people continued to work in the fields—tending crops such as tobacco, shown here in North Carolina—and still had to report to a white man, but now he was the employer rather than the master.

agricultural and domestic work environment thus set the scene for struggles between freed people and their employers over their conflicting definitions of free labor.

As 1865 ended, freed people were becoming reluctant to work for white employers because at that time they expected to receive their own land from the federal government. As one man argued, "Gib us our own land and we take care of ourselves; but widout land, de ole massas can hire us or starve us as dey please." And after refusing to work for 25 cents a day for his former owner, another worker declared, "I mean to own my own manhood, and I'm goin' on to my own land, just as soon as when I git dis crop in, an' I don't desire for to many change until den.... I'm not goin' to work for any man for any such price." Freed people argued that they deserved the land because they had never been paid for their labor as slaves. "We have build up their houses and cultivated their lands," one African American minister argued. "If they [employers] were to pay us but twenty-five cents on the dollar, they would all be very poor." One man in Alabama summed up the feelings of many freed people to a Union soldier: "The property which they hold was nearly all earned by the sweat of *our* brows." Appealing a decision to remove African Americans from land in Virginia, one quasi landowner defiantly pleaded: "We has a right to the land where we are located. . . . Our wives, our children, our husbands, has been sold over and over again to purchase the lands we now locates upon; for that reason we have a divine right to the land." Years after the war another man argued that "they should have give us part of Maser's land as us poor old slaves we made what our Masers had."

Despite such requests, President Johnson returned to the former slave owners the land the freed people had gained during the war. Most white Northerners agreed with Johnson's decision to advocate wage labor rather than land ownership for former slaves. They believed that land confiscation was too radical a practice for the federal government to promote. Agents from the Freedmen's Bureau therefore traveled throughout the South explaining that the government was not, in fact, going to distribute land. These agents also insisted on having labor contracts between employers and freed people in order to provide fair wages and working conditions for employees and give planters a reliable labor force. Such contracts were agreements between workers and employers indicating wages to be paid and the kind of work to be performed. Other clauses were often included as well, such as statements on deportment. In one case, workers were "required to be orderly industrious people and observe the rules of the place." Contracts also restricted when workers could have guests, as in stipulations such as "no neighboring negroes will be allowed to remain in the quarters [housing for former slaves] longer than 12 hours, without reporting to [the employer]."

At first, African Americans resisted signing labor contracts because they wanted to hold out for owning their own land. They were afraid of "signing them[selves] back to their masters" as one Freedmen's Bureau agent said. A freedman declared, ""If I can't own de land, I'll hire or lease land, but I won't contract." Hoping for more economic independence from whites, some African Americans organized to protest these year-long labor contracts. Other freed people tried to exist on abandoned lands, as self-employed families, by planting crops, hunting, and fishing.

With or without labor contracts, freed people eventually began to

A white employer of black sharecroppers rides through the cotton fields to check their work, much as he might have done when he controlled these workers as slaves.

STATE OF ARKANSAS,
County of Pulaski } ss.

KNOW ALL MEN BY THESE PRESENTS.

THAT WE, the undersigned Employer, party of the first part, and the undersigned Employees, parties of the second part, are held and firmly bound unto each other in the following CONTRACT, to begin January 1st 186_ and expire December 31st 1866.

I. The party of the first part, for and in consideration of the stipulations of the parties of the second part, agree to furnish the parties of the second part, and each of them, full and substantial rations, sufficient fuel and quarters, and all needful medicine and medical attendance during the continuance of this contract; and to pay each of the parties of the second part, the amount set opposite their respective names per month; said amount to be paid in full on or before the expiration of this contract, or at the final disposal of the crop, if it should be disposed of prior to the expiration of this contract.

II. The parties of the second part, for and in consideration of the stipulations of the part y of the first part, agree to render to the party of the first part, good and faithful service, to be performed under the direction of the employer, or that of his agent, and not to be absent from the place of employment in working hours without permission, unless treated with cruelty. And the parties of the second part do each of them further agree to work twenty-six days*

(No loss of time for rainy weather)

for a month's labor; and to forfeit to the part of the first part their pay and the value of their rations, for so much of their time as they fail to perform their part of this contract; provided such failure or loss of time shall be reported at the end of each month to the Agent or Superintendent of the Freedmen's Bureau and be verified by him.

Witness our hand and seal this 5th day of January 186_

T. S. Hobbs { Employer, part of the first part.

* Here the parties can fix the time to constitute a day's work.

EMPLOYEES PARTIES OF THE SECOND PART.					
NAMES.	AGE.	Rate of Pay per Month. Doll's Cts.	NAMES.	AGE.	Rate of Pay per Month. Doll's Cts.
Jacob Kimball	26	20 00	Peter Travis	20	20 00
Barbara Young	24	16 00	Wm Keating	20	20 00
Henry Thomas	20	20 00	Amanda Brown	18	16 00
Walter Madison	37	20 00	Charlotte Jones	18	16 00
Lawson Winford	15	12 00	Randall Jones	40	24 00
Eda Connor	30	16 00	Obram Hill	35	20 00
Eola Hill	24	16 00	Ave Winfrey	24	20 00
Adeline Connor	30	16 00	Dan Jackson	60	16 00
Manida Finley	25	16 00	William Johnson		
Mary Winfrey	19	16 00	Martha Marshall		
Jane Mack	18	16 00			
Andrew Huff	17	15 00			
Mary Ann Travis	26	16 00			
Eda Connor	18	15 00			
Miami Connor	15	12 00			
Ann Hill	20	16 00			
Amanda Connor	16	15 00			
Wesley Connor	12	10 00			
R. W. Robinson	25	20 00			
Thos. Gordon	16	15 00			
Ernst Reynolds	30	20 00			
Jefferson Alder	20	20 00			
Wm Bender	25	20 00			
Isaac Wassal	17	16 00			
David Pennington	18	16 00			
Raymond Wassal	60	4 00			
Harriet Brown	28	15 00			

A one-year labor contract lists (on the right) the names of employees, their age, and monthly pay. The left page stipulates that this Arkansas planter must provide his workers with food, fuel, and living quarters in addition to their monthly pay.

work for white employers simply because they were poor and needed the work. And as part of the Black Codes, state governments passed vagrancy laws that punished African Americans by jailing them if they were not employed by a white person. Even when pressured into working for wages, freed people resisted as much as they could. Workers turned the yearly signing of labor contracts into negotiating sessions in which they discussed working arrangements. They held out as long as possible to work out the best deals. Immediately after the war, labor shortages developed in the South that not only kept wages competitive but also allowed laborers to gain extra concessions, such as the right to keep their own garden patch and to have more say in managing the plantation.

The majority of the freed men and women worked in the fields growing cotton, rice, and other crops. Planters continued to need

Children grind rice in Charleston, South Carolina. Most freed people in the South continued to work in the fields; agriculture was the area's primary industry.

agricultural workers, but few postwar Southern households employed as many house servants as they had previously. Former slave owners hired some freedwomen as maids and cooks, but the contracts show that they also performed other work related to food production. One woman, for instance, agreed in her labor contract "to do cooking, washing, ironing, and general housework and anything about the yard or garden that may be required of her." Another, Lucy Davis, cooked, milked the cow, and washed and ironed clothes for one white family. Charity Riley's employers expected her to do the dairying (including making the butter), feed the chickens, cook, wash, and spin and weave cloth. When needed, house servants went out into the fields, especially at harvest or cotton-picking time.

Wages for agricultural workers varied. Monthly wages ranged from $10 to $20 for men and $8 to $10 for women and children older than 12. These wages did not buy very much. For example, one freedwoman bought a bar of soap for 50 cents from a store located on the plantation where she was working. This purchase alone probably represented 5 percent of her monthly income. Often the sugar plantations paid the highest wages because the owners were paid better prices for this crop than others. Some planters calculated a monthly wage and would agree to pay with cash only when they sold the crops. Other farmers paid by giving workers a share of the crop, which the employer usually sold after harvesting. He would then divide the money between himself and the workers. Shares for the work force ranged from one-half to one-quarter of the crop. Occasionally, planters would give the workers' share of the crop directly to them and let them divide it among themselves. At first, planters used the same labor contract for many workers, whether they were related or not. Over time, however, contracts became narrower, with only one family per contract.

Initially, the former slave owners anticipated ruling their employees with the same authority masters had exercised over slaves. Despite their acceptance of the demise of slavery, they could not accept a free labor system in which African Americans would be able to exercise the same rights as whites, such as changing employment or working without physical coercion. As a result, employers sometimes reacted violently to any challenge to their dominance. As one Mississippi newspaper summarized the attitude of most former slave owners, "The true station of the negro is that of a servant. The wants and state of our country demand that he should remain a servant."

A black maid cares for a white child around 1883. The majority of black women worked either as agricultural laborers or as domestic servants for white families.

The freed people believed, however, that they were entitled to protest labor conditions they considered unfair. Workers and employers argued not only over wages but also about nonpayment of wages. The latter represented the largest number of complaints brought to the Freedmen's Bureau by freed people. As one argued, "I craves work, ma'am, if I gets a little pay, but if we don't gets pay, we don't care—don't care to work." To justify not paying workers their wages, planters typically used the defense that the laborers had bought items in the employer-owned stores on the plantations and had in this way already spent their wages. Employers also deducted stiff fines for missed work, as much as 50 cents or $1 a day. This rate was often much higher than what employees were paid per day. Freed men and women complained that their employers routinely found trivial excuses to dismiss them after the harvest, to avoid paying them. Since they lived where they worked, when planters ordered laborers off the plantations, the workers lost their homes as well as their jobs.

The former slave owners' reluctance to accept the loss of restrictions on workers such as had existed under slavery was compounded by their own economic difficulties. They had, in fact, very little money to pay their workers with, in part because after the war the federal government declared the Confederate dollar worthless. Even before the war,

This 1867 illustration by Thomas Nast is entitled Whipping a Negro Girl in North Carolina by "Unreconstructed" Johnsonians. *Some whites insisted that blacks needed to be disciplined, as they had under slavery, before they would do satisfactory work.*

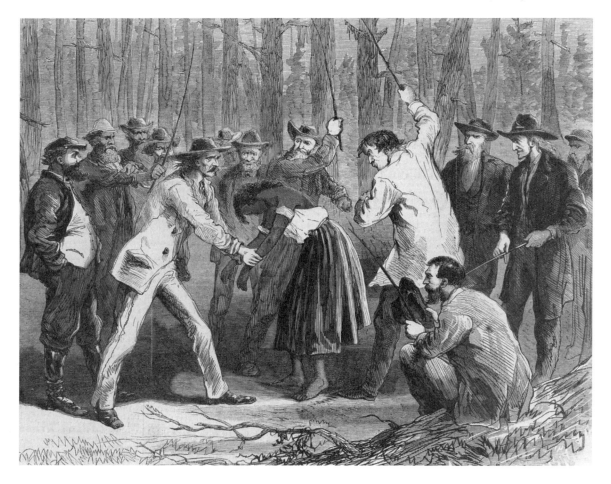

The ruins of once-beautiful Columbia, South Carolina, at the end of the Civil War. Such devastation of land and property imposed hardship on both blacks and whites as they struggled to rebuild the South after the war.

much of the planters' wealth had depended on their slaves and land. The planters lost their slaves without compensation, and in parts of the South some of the land and property was ruined by the war. In general, land values declined after the war. On top of this, the years 1866 and 1867 witnessed agricultural disaster throughout many areas of the South. Bad weather and an invasion of army worms, which are particularly voracious caterpillars, contributed to crop failures. In 1867 and 1868 when cotton prices decreased from wartime highs (although not to the levels of pre-war prices), interest rates rose as planters' ability to borrow tightened. Planters were often in debt to merchants for their supplies.

Planters often proved unable to pay their workers or were unwilling to share the very small profits they had achieved at the end of the year. Given these financial woes, planters wanted a docile labor force willing to work for low wages. Employers were convinced that African Americans would not work without being compelled to through stringent vagrancy laws, restrictive labor contracts, and the threatened use of the whip. Whites saw work as labor for white employers, not African-American self-employment. They feared economically independent African Americans because they believed they would be harder to control.

As Democrats regained majorities in Southern state legislatures, they passed laws that helped planters assert authority over African-American workers. They enacted legislation that made it more difficult for workers to get paid by allowing planters to pay merchants and other creditors before paying their laborers. Furthermore, to keep African Americans more financially dependent on planters and merchants, laws were passed that limited their rights to hunt and fish. During Reconstruction, the Ku Klux Klan perpetrated violence against workers if it thought that they were not sufficiently subservient to whites. The Klan especially targeted African Americans who were self-employed and therefore not dependent on whites. As one freedman explained, the Klan "do not like to see the negro go ahead."

Besides difficulties over the payment of wages, conflicts erupted between freed people and planters over how work should be done and

A black couple plows through their corn-field without benefit of a mule. Most freed people did not own their own land after the war but engaged in a sharecropping arrangement, which often prevented them from ever saving enough money to buy their own plots of land.

when. The former slave owners wanted their workers to labor in groups referred to as "gangs." During slavery, a white overseer supervised the work of these gangs, often with the help of one slave, called a driver. After the war, planters hired men they referred to as agents or foremen to do the work of overseers. Workers resented these agents (even in the rare cases where they were African American) and refused to work in the field with them. One planter reported that his workers told him, "We won't be driven by nobody." Another protested, "I don't want no driving, either by a black man or white man." Freed people insisted on working in smaller groups, often with family members, without continual white oversight.

In addition to resisting working in gangs under close supervision from whites, blacks also protested the use of violence, such as whipping, to discipline workers. Although labor contracts often forbade whippings, many white employers were convinced that blacks needed the threat of violence to make them work. As one planter insisted, "They can't be governed except with the whip."

Workers protested their conditions in various tangible ways. Some joined together to resist violent behavior. In Mississippi, when one overseer tried to harm a field worker, the others turned on him so that he "had to run for [his] life," according to his testimony to the congressional Joint Committee on Reconstruction. One planter's wife wrote about a group of workers who reacted to abuse perpetrated by an employer's son by becoming "a howling, cursing mob with the women shrieking, 'Kill him!' and all brandishing pistols and guns." The son was quickly sent to a private school away from the plantation.

In July 1876, workers in the rice fields of South Carolina went out on strike because the planters had paid them with pieces of paper called scrip that could be redeemed only in plantation stores. These stores often had higher prices than outside places. Feeling cheated, the workers wanted the freedom to make their own decisions about how and where to spend their wages. This strike ended in partial victory for the laborers. Although the strike organizers were jailed, the planters agreed to stop paying their workers only in scrip.

Freed African Americans now refused to perform labor not expressly negotiated in their contracts or not associated with the actual raising of the crops. For instance, some freed people resisted repairing fencing or feeding livestock. They demanded opportunities to make more

U.S. Representative Robert Smalls (inset) sent his account of the South Carolina rice strike to the governor; in it, he condemned the planters' system of paying workers with scrip rather than money.

Beaufort S C Aug 24th 1876

To His Excellency
        Gov D H Chamberlain
                Columbia S.C

Sir;

I recieved a telegram from the Attorny General to call out the Millitia, if necessary; to put down the riot on the Combahee. I proceeded yester-day to the disturbed rice districts and found no rioters, nor had there been a riot; but I did find a large body of men numbering about three hundred who had refused to work for checks. a sample of which you will find in-closed.   The cause of the strike was that the rice planters issued these checks instead of money, and that they are only redeemed in goods that must be purchased at exorbitant prices at the stores of the planters, and the whole amount taken in goods, or change given in checks, thus making it impossibee for the decisions about the crop they were raising, particularly when they were working for a share of it. They wanted to decide early on with the planter how much of each crop to plant and when and where to sell it. Planters preferred waiting until the end of the year to pay them, however, to help ensure that the workers performed noncrop-related labor during the rest of the year.

Planters continued to believe, as Major Martin Delaney pointed out, that freed people did not work as hard as they might. But increasingly, they came to realize that giving laborers a share of the crop was a better incentive than contracting with them for cash. When signing labor contracts, freed people tried to negotiate for the form of payment they preferred. For example, freed people who never received the cash wages they were promised wanted a share of the crop, feeling more assured of such payment.

Disputes also developed over freed people's intention to work fewer hours than they had as slaves. They resisted working from sunup to sundown. They now began to demand Saturday as well as Sunday as days off. Besides working for their regular earnings, freed people cultivated gardens or sometimes rented a small plot of land to raise vegetables and other crops to sell on their own. Having fewer hours of field work provided new spare time for such activities. Freed people also came to expect to spend more time with their families, friends, and neighbors. Although planters opposed any changes from slave conditions, freed people expected the needs of their families to be considered in decisions on how much time freedwomen and children should devote to outside employment. African Americans now wanted their children to go to school, not work in the fields.

Freedwomen's tasks for their families increased after the war. Under slavery, breakfast and dinner were often eaten in the fields. The master would typically designate an elderly black woman to look after all the children while their parents worked. Moreover, with freedom, cooking and making clothes now often ceased to be communal activities.

Besides doing the cooking, washing, sewing, and gardening, freedwomen took charge of caring for their own children. Pregnant and nursing mothers wanted to give up outside work. Mothers sometimes argued with their employers about giving their babies more attention instead of working in the fields. One planter complained in his journal,

Women wash clothes outdoors, under South Carolina pines, around 1880. Although they engaged in such communal activities, freedwomen tried to spend as much time as possible with their own families, caring for children and husbands.

"Harriet and Amelia nursing over 12 months, disobeyed order to quit suckling [nursing]." A few planters even reacted violently against mothers who spent more time with their families than employers allowed. William Jenkins, the employer and former master of a freedwoman named Annette, once whipped her because she arrived late to work. When Jenkins ordered her to strip off her clothes for the beating, she pleaded, "Master William I had my children to tend to made me so late." Jenkins then gave her 200 lashes with his rawhide whip. Clearly he had not yet made the transition from a slavery mentality to one of freedom.

Freedwomen's need to spend more time with their children without constant interference from white employers was only one of the factors that encouraged the growth of postwar sharecropping. Sharecropping spread at different rates in different parts of the South. It was often preceded by other labor experiments, including monetary wage contracts and the practice of working in small groups referred to as squads. Sharecropping usually involved a planter's paying his workers a part of the crop, up to as much as half, for their labor. The planter generally provided the tools and seed.

Sharecropping developed because freed people did not receive land and because employers often failed to pay promised wages on a regular basis. For freed people, sharecropping also meant less direct supervision by white overseers and the ability to work in units smaller than gangs. It allowed women to balance their time between field work and doing their own families' domestic tasks. Under sharecropping, freedmen could make more choices about how to use their family resources and labor. Freed people also tried to arrange their field work so that their children were able to attend school. The planters ultimately came to accept sharecropping, although they preferred the gang system of labor under the supervision of a white overseer.

Although sharecropping allowed freed people more independence than they had under slavery, it had severe drawbacks. Since sharecroppers bought their food, clothing, and other items from the plantation store, they often finished the year in debt or with very little profit. And as cotton prices fell, sharecropping increasingly became economically devastating for African Americans, poor whites, and the South as a whole. As one freedman summed it up, his people had received "freedom without giving us any chance to live to ourselves and we still had to depend on the southern white man for work, food, and clothing, and he held us through our necessity and want in a state of servitude but little better than slavery." As another wrote, "No man can work another man's land . . . even for half and board and clothe himself and family and make any money. The consequence will be the freedmen will become poorer and poorer every year."

Many of the newly freed wanted to leave their plantations to seek out better economic opportunities and education for their children. However, when they migrated into either Southern or Northern cities following the war, they found the employment opportunities very limited. Often, the men found jobs as blacksmiths, bricklayers, or carpenters if

Workers in the fields on St. Helena Island, off the South Carolina coast, around 1866. Although sharecropping was definitely an improvement over slavery, for many blacks it was an unsatisfactory arrangement because it required them to be dependent on a white landowner.

they had done these jobs as slaves. They also found work as barbers and as waiters in restaurants and hotels. The Republican party helped some African Americans gain politically appointed jobs as postal clerks, mail carriers, deputy sheriffs, county clerks, and customs workers. A few blacks attempted to start their own businesses, but many of these failed in the wake of the depression of 1873. Freedwomen typically became domestics and washerwomen.

African-American men, like other Americans, looked to the West for better employment opportunities. Although they found more diverse types of employment in the West than in the North or South, they also faced discrimination. As African-American men moved West during Reconstruction, they joined cattle drives as cooks and cowboys and drove

Kitchen workers employed by Harvard University in 1875, with aprons over their suits. Serving whites—as waiters, bellhops, or barbers, for example—was generally the only kind of work open to many of the black men who left the South after the war.

cattle in Kansas and Texas. According to his book, Nat Love, who drove cattle, earned the nickname Deadwood Dick by winning a roping contest in Deadwood, Arizona. Some African Americans became farmers in the West by taking advantage of the Homestead Act, which offered free land to those who agreed to cultivate it. Others went west as soldiers. In 1866 the U.S. Army formed African-American regiments of the 9th and 10th Cavalry and organized the 24th and 25th Infantry in 1869. The troops went west and southwest to protect the settlers moving out there. They also built roads, constructed telegraph lines, captured cattle rustlers, protected workers constructing the railroads, and guarded the mail. African-American men tried other kinds of employment in the West and Southwest, such as becoming railroad workers and miners, because these jobs paid more than field work. In San Francisco, where most African Americans were single males, men worked as sailors and railroad personnel. Black women in western cities were still primarily limited to domestic work; some found employment as laundresses.

Some African-American men in the West became very successful. In 1865, blacks in San Francisco owned tobacco and soap factories as well as laundries and real estate offices. A few men formed mining companies, such as the Colored Citizens of California. African Americans also owned silver mines in Nevada, Montana, Colorado, and Utah. In 1870, Clara Brown, who cooked and washed for miners, became the first African-American member of the Colorado Pioneer Association. A few African-American entrepreneurs were quite successful, including the founders of the Cosmopolitan Coal & Wood Company.

Increasingly, after the war—in both the North and the West—black skilled workers like carpenters, blacksmiths, and barbers, who often had received their training during slavery, found that gaining employment was difficult. White employers did not want to hire them, partly because white workers, fearing the competition of blacks, often refused to work with them. On occasion, whites hired African Americans to replace better-paid whites or used African Americans as strikebreakers, which promoted racial hostility. In 1865, white workers in Baltimore drove off African-American carpenters and caulkers from their jobs. Another reason white employers did not hire blacks was that they preferred to rely on the labor of immigrants, who were considered easier to control. Skilled African-American workers were often therefore forced into unskilled labor, doing the lowest-paying, dirtiest, least skilled jobs. By 1870, most African Americans were unskilled laborers or service workers.

Lack of union support also increased the labor difficulties of skilled African Americans. Unions often refused to allow blacks to join, although a few did organize segregated locals, which separated white and African-American workers. Typical was the experience of Lewis Douglass, the son of Frederick Douglass. Lewis Douglass was prohibited from joining the Typographical Union in Washington, D.C., even though he had worked in his father's print shop and had excellent experience. The inability to join a union kept African-American youth from apprenticing themselves to skilled workers and learning a trade. In December 1869, the National Negro Labor Union was established to enable African Americans to join a union and fight for better wages and working conditions. The great majority of African-American workers, however, even

In Charleston, workers shovel coal. Such unskilled labor was often the only choice for black men, who faced discrimination by white employers.

Employees in an oyster-processing plant in 1872. Black women often had to work outside the home to support their families.

those living in the cities, remained outside unions.

In cities as well as the countryside, white employers paid African-American workers less than whites. Tobacco factory workers in Richmond, Virginia, complained that "we the Tobacco mechanicks of this city and Manchester is worked to great disadvantage. . . . They say we will starve through laziness that is not so. But it is true we will starve at our present wages." Collective action by African-American workers such as washerwomen and day laborers to protest their low wages and poor working conditions was not uncommon. African-American urban workers organized strikes, but they often failed to achieve either higher wages or better working conditions.

During Reconstruction, African Americans were ultimately unable to fulfill their dreams of economic independence. Poor agricultural conditions, labor restrictions, legal and illegal discrimination, failure to obtain land, and the worsening economic times during the depression of 1873 guaranteed poverty for the majority of Southern African Americans. The economic plight of the nation's freed people represented one of Reconstruction's biggest failures.

CHAPTER 5

FAMILY: "MY NAME WAS PEGGIE ONE OF THE CHILDREN OF PRINCE AND ROSE"

◇ ◇ ◇

Freedwoman Maria Clark recalled in some detail her relationship with her husband, specifically how it began during slavery and survived the war: "I had been with my young mistress about three years when I married Henry Clark in 1859, I fix the date by knowing it was about two years before the late war broke out. My Master performed the marriage ceremony, he did not give me or my husband papers to show for our marriage, but gave us a great treat for all the slaves on the plantation." The couple "remained on the Clark Plantation in Hinds County [Mississippi] thru [the] battle of Vicksburg end[ing] in 1863, which was the first time we knew we were free, all the slaves in the surrounding county was gathered into a camp on a plantation about five miles from Vicksburg."

Henry and Maria Clark stayed in the contraband camp until Henry and many of the other men were enlisted in the Union army. Maria then followed her husband into the army to cook for the soldiers. "When the troops moved off many of us were sent upon the Paw Paw Island where I rented ground to make my living in his absence. I received news that he was very sick in [a] Hospital at Memphis, Tenn. As soon as I could raise money I went there with the determination to take care of him, when I arrived there I found him some better." Clark was discharged soon after his wife arrived and she took him home, although he was "very weak and

To live with and care for one's own family without fear of separation—something that had been denied to slaves—was a goal for blacks after the war. This family was photographed in 1886.

A slave family on a South Carolina plantation in 1862. On large plantations, families were often able to stay together, but they lived with the fear of being sold away.

complained of great suffering. While on the journey, when the boat struck the landing at Paw Paw Island we met several of our friends, who were acquainted with him before he entered the service they assisted me in getting him from the boat." Clark died six months later.

As Maria Clark's narrative shows, slavery did not destroy all African-American families. Some slave couples remained devoted to each other in spite of hardship, even though slave marriages were not legal. Such marriages provided the foundation for many African-American families after the war.

Even though slave masters had the right to separate the members of slave families by selling them, many families nevertheless developed strong ties. The strength of these families can be seen in the desperate hunting after the war when wives, husbands, and children sought each other. Freed people wrote to the Freedmen's Bureau requesting information about the location of their family members. Freedman Moses Norman wanted "information of the whereabouts of his sister" because he was "anxious to have her come and live with him." Another inquirer, Frances Bell, wanted to know about her children, who had been slaves in

North Carolina, because she had "great anxiety regarding their welfare." And years after being sold away from her family, Peggy Kelly wrote to her former owner asking about her parents, sisters, and brothers. She pleaded, "Any information given if any of the whereabouts of them will be thankfully rec'd. Let me know if they are dead or alive. My name was Peggie one of the children of Prince and Rose."

Even though couples could not legally marry during slavery, slave families sustained each other through the day-to-day rigors of slavery. Slave couples participated in marriage ceremonies, often with permission of the masters, who sometimes allowed slave weddings to be held on holidays such as the Fourth of July. But the three-day Christmas holiday, which most masters gave as time off from work, was the favorite time to get married. The weddings of house slaves were often quite elaborate, with food and dancing. When a slave named Susan Drane married fellow slave Charles Hooven, a white preacher conducted the ceremony in the owner's parlor. The event was attended by the master's family "and a number of invited guests. They had a grand supper upon the occasion." At some ceremonies the master read from the Bible.

Slaves, possibly belonging to Jefferson Davis, participate in a wedding celebration on Davis Island, Mississippi. Some masters condoned such ceremonies, but the marriages were not legally binding.

Some slaves did not have a wedding ceremony. One formerly enslaved father remembered that when his daughter married a man from another plantation, "I gave my consent and both the owners agreeing, he came on a certain night and they went to bed together and after that time he visited and cohabitated with her as his wife." He added that "there was no formal ceremony, but they considered themselves husband and wife and were so regarded by others." The father recalled that he had been married the same way as his daughter.

Slavery constantly threatened such marriages. The marriage registers of freed people kept by the Freedmen's Bureau have provided an indication of how long slave marriages generally lasted. One historian has determined that approximately 18 percent of slave marriages ended involuntarily. Others have calculated that almost 39 percent of slave marriages were "broken by the master."

Emancipation brought legalized marriage to the formerly enslaved couples. During the Civil War, African-American couples kept Union army chaplains busy performing marriage ceremonies. Lucinda Westbrooks recalled being "married by a white man preacher Miller— who came there with the first Yankees and went around marrying the soldiers. He married lots of other soldiers the same day." Chaplains often held soldiers' weddings for several couples at once. At one army camp, the chaplain conducted a group marriage ceremony, after which everyone in the army camp celebrated with "a wedding feast . . . that night and all the boys of the company were at it," according to one soldier. Freed people referred to legal marriages as marriages "under the flag." Army regulations promoted such marriages because the military allowed only legally married spouses to visit soldiers.

After the war, couples delighted in the festivities accompanying weddings, either for new couples or as second weddings for those who had been married during slavery. Freed people viewed their slave marriages as binding even after emancipation. However, the Freedmen's Bureau discounted slave marriages because they had not been legal and regarded these new weddings as celebrating first marriages.

African Americans' reasons for wanting to marry after the war varied. For many, marriages symbolized freedom because they no longer needed a master's permission. Legalized marriage also meant that children now belonged to their mother and father and could not be sold.

In this advertisement for slaves to be auctioned, family members have been pointed out but separated by different item numbers so that they can be offered for sale individually.

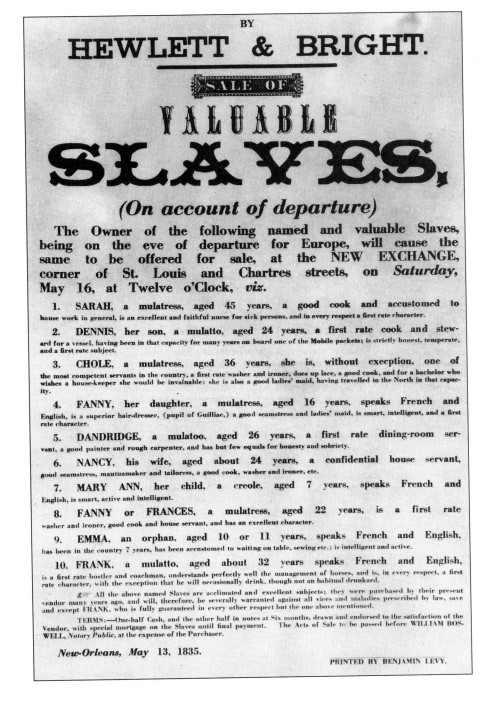

BY

HEWLETT & BRIGHT.

SALE OF

VALUABLE SLAVES,

(On account of departure)

The Owner of the following named and valuable Slaves, being on the eve of departure for Europe, will cause the same to be offered for sale, at the NEW EXCHANGE, corner of St. Louis and Chartres streets, on *Saturday,* May 16, at Twelve o'Clock, *viz.*

1. **SARAH**, a mulatress, aged 45 years, a good cook and accustomed to house work in general, is an excellent and faithful nurse for sick persons, and in every respect a first rate character.

2. **DENNIS**, her son, a mulatto, aged 24 years, a first rate cook and steward for a vessel, having been in that capacity for many years on board one of the Mobile packets; is strictly honest, temperate, and a first rate subject.

3. **CHOLE**, a mulatress, aged 36 years, she is, without exception, one of the most competent servants in the country, a first rate washer and ironer, does up lace, a good cook, and for a bachelor who wishes a house-keeper she would be invaluable: she is also a good ladies' maid, having travelled to the North in that capacity.

4. **FANNY**, her daughter, a mulatress, aged 16 years, speaks French and English, is a superior hair-dresser, (pupil of Guilliac,) a good seamstress and ladies' maid, is smart, intelligent, and a first rate character.

5. **DANDRIDGE**, a mulatoo, aged 26 years, a first rate dining-room servant, a good painter and rough carpenter, and has but few equals for honesty and sobriety.

6. **NANCY**, his wife, aged about 24 years, a confidential house servant, good seamstress, mantuamaker and tailoress, a good cook, washer and ironer, etc.

7. **MARY ANN**, her child, a creole, aged 7 years, speaks French and English, is smart, active and intelligent.

8. **FANNY or FRANCES**, a mulatress, aged 22 years, is a first rate washer and ironer, good cook and house servant, and has an excellent character.

9. **EMMA**, an orphan, aged 10 or 11 years, speaks French and English, has been in the country 7 years, has been accustomed to waiting on table, sewing etc.: is intelligent and active.

10. **FRANK**, a mulatto, aged about 32 years speaks French and English, is a first rate hostler and coachman, understands perfectly well the management of horses, and is, in every respect, a first rate character, with the exception that he will occasionally drink, though not an habitual drunkard.

☞ All the above named Slaves are acclimated and excellent subjects; they were purchased by their present vendor many years ago, and will, therefore, be severally warranted against all vices and maladies prescribed by law, save and except FRANK, who is fully guaranteed in every other respect but the one above mentioned.

TERMS:—One-half Cash, and the other half in notes at Six months, drawn and endorsed to the satisfaction of the Vendor, with special mortgage on the Slaves until final payment. The Acts of Sale to be passed before WILLIAM BOSWELL, *Notary Public,* at the expense of the Purchaser.

New-Orleans, May 13, 1835.

PRINTED BY BENJAMIN LEVY.

Furthermore, church membership often required legalized marriage. The First African Baptist Church of New Orleans, for one, passed such a policy after the abolition of slavery, declaring, "Any person wishing to become members of this church who may be living in a state of illegitimate marriage shall first procure a license and marry." As one woman recalled, "We got married by license, because the church we joined required every one to be married by license." Many freed people marrying after the Civil War sought out a church with an African-American congregation and preacher. As one Freedmen's Bureau official wrote in 1865, freed people "all manifest a disposition to marry in the church, and prefer a minister of the Gospel to unite them."

Former slaves acquired a second family during slavery if they were sold and then remarried. These circumstances, as well as other marital problems often made worse by poverty, caused abandonment by spouses. Desertion brought about particularly serious consequences for African-American women with children. In one case, Nathan Williams, after nine

The First African Baptist Church of Richmond, Virginia, was established in 1865. Black congregations became a powerful force in communities after the war.

years of marriage to his wife, Louisa, left her and "married again leaving her with one child without means of support," according to a Freedmen's Bureau agent. Such abandonments could be emotionally painful for the spouse left behind. Once a Northerner inquired of a freedwoman, "You have no husband?" The woman responded, "I had one . . . but he ran away one day with another woman. . . . Feel like it most killed me at first. I get over it now."

Marital disagreements occasionally led to domestic violence. When this happened, African-American women felt justified in leaving abusive husbands. One black woman named Amanda Fay had a slave husband who, according to her pension examiner, used to "whip her and treat her roughly," so "she quit him because he treated her badly, and; because she thought she had a perfect right to [do] so." Similarly, Emma Daily refused to live with her husband because of his abuse. Often, members of the extended family would intervene in marriages when violence became a pronounced problem. One mother asked her employer to separate her daughter and her son-in-law because he beat her daughter. And one wife, having been assaulted by her husband, complained to her father about the beating. Her father and brother confronted the husband, demanding that he stop the abuse. An argument ensued, and the woman's brother shot her husband in the leg.

While thousands of men and women married as slaves later remarried, some African Americans chose not to go through a formal marriage ceremony. Some refused to marry because a new marriage would jeopardize the woman's pension from the U.S. government. When Union soldiers died, whether during or after their service, their widows were entitled to a pension, or payment, from the government. These widows' pension ($8 a month for a private's wife) sometimes made women reluctant to remarry after a husband's death. The federal laws relating to the dispensation of pensions forbade women who remarried or lived with a man from claiming a military pension. Some widows believed they could hide the reality of their living with a man more easily than they could disguise remarriage because cohabitation did not create records such as a marriage certificate. In one instance, two years after her husband died, freedwoman Louisa Smith began living with a man named Abraham Speers. As she explained, "I have never married Speers because I understood that by marrying I would lose my right to pension."

As in Smith's case, such relationships after the war were just like marriages, except that they were not legalized. Couples lived together, with the woman adopting her man's surname. They cared about each other's well-being, and they were sexually intimate. After explaining that she and Thomas Toller had never married but had "lived together until he died," from 1866 to 1904, freedwoman Isabella Toller elaborated, "I had the name Carter and was called Isabella Toller and have not been called or known by any other name since." She noted that when their first child was born, "It was his child and he said it was and we agreed, he and I and my mother, that we would go together for all time." As soon as the pension office discovered these relationships, through intensive questioning of whites or African Americans who knew the women, they ceased paying pensions to them.

When a freedman did marry, he became the legal head of the family. During slavery, the slave masters had held all legal rights to slave

A free family in front of its log-cabin home. After the war, African-American men became the legal heads of their households.

Black women, like most white women, were responsible for the housework and child care in their homes, while the husband assumed the role of provider and head of the household.

families, including the power to sell family members. Even so, a slave father played a part in his family's life. When the master distributed blankets or clothing, for example, to the head of each slave family, the slave father rather than mother usually received them if the couple lived together on the same plantation. Slave men also held leadership positions on plantations as drivers, artisans, and preachers.

After slavery, the freedman, as husband and father, rather than the master assumed legal responsibility for his family, including guardianship of his children. When employers refused to pay their wives or drove their families off of plantations, husbands represented their family members before the Freedmen's Bureau agent or in court. Men tried to protect their spouses and children, particularly from beatings by employers. One freedman defended his shooting of a white man by arguing that the man had "abused [his] wife." Sometimes men signed labor contracts for the entire family and received the whole family's wages. Increasingly, after the war, employers put labor contracts and accounts at the plantation store in the husband's name, even when other members of the family also worked there.

After the war, freedmen greatly expanded the economic responsibilities they assumed for their families. According to testimony from a pension examiner, one freedman began thinking about his new role while serving in the army: "He had a chance to marry in the service, but could not take care of a wife like he ought to in the army, and did not marry." Four years after the end of the war, once he found work, he did marry. One will left by a freedman showed the extent to which men thought of their wives' economic well-being. Although few freed people left such documents because they often lacked property and were illiterate, freedman Daniel Sanders dictated a will to his employer. He directed that "after my burial expenses are satisfied and all of my just debts are paid which is few I will all I have to go to my wife Leather as long as she lives, And then to be disposed of as she may see fit." Sanders also made provision for his wife's grandson. The Sanders estate "consist[ed] of one mule, one cow, and some debts due me."

Men and women performed different tasks for their families. Freedwomen took on more child care than they had during slavery. They also did such household work as cooking, washing clothes, and cleaning the houses or cabins. Although freed men and women considered the husband the main provider in the family, freedwomen also worked, either as field laborers or as domestic servants for white families. A freedwoman's contributions were important to the welfare of her family. Women sometimes raised vegetables or other crops for the family outside of any wage labor or a sharecropping arrangement. For example, in 1868, when Robert Shackleford signed a contract concerning yearly wages for himself and his sons, the employer also agreed "to let the wife of said Robert Shackleford have for cultivation a certain piece of land . . . for her sole care and benefit" as well as land for a garden.

Purchase records from plantation stores reflect the differences in men's and women's family activities as well as distinctions in their dress. In January 1868, on the Oakwood plantation in Mississippi, men bought pants, caps, shirts, boots, and hunting and fishing gear like shot, fishing line, powder, hooks, and buckets. Women purchased material for clothes making like cotton plaid, but no pants or shirts. Men and women both bought whiskey, tobacco, lamp oil, and thread. Freedwomen wore dresses, or skirts and blouses for field labor, while African-American men wore pants and shirts. Women decorated their outfits by adding ribbons and, when they could afford it, enjoyed wearing jewelry, often buying earrings. They willingly spent part of their pay on their attire. Freed-

In this 1879 painting, a black woman and her children tend to a garden beside their cabin. Women often had to do something extra, such as maintain a garden or work outside the home, to help provide for their families.

woman Hattie Jefferson purchased a dress upon receiving her first wages for picking cotton. Women elaborately styled their hair by wrapping it with strips of cloth, particularly on special occasions. Wrapping hair and wearing decorative handkerchiefs were both African traditions.

Whites often ignored a freedman's place as head of a family. When husbands who had been separated from their families either by slavery or

war returned, whites often resisted their efforts to reclaim their families. Employers did not want men reuniting with their families if it meant losing workers before harvest time. In one case, Bill Price's wife's employer shot at him when he tried to move his family away from the plantation. The local courts then ignored Price's complaints about forced separation of his family as well as the violence. And Freedman Abram Munice charged his wife's employer with "the unlawful detention of his wife and four children." Munice wanted his family to leave Mississippi and join him in Memphis, Tennessee. Such cases caused one Freedmen's Bureau agent to complain about former slave owners who continued after the war to believe they had the power to "part man and wife and bid defiance of God and man."

Whites, particularly employers, refused to recognize either the right of freed people to form independent families or African-American women's right to choose their own sexual partners. Along with attempts to keep family members separated, white men sometimes sexually abused black women. On occasion, although less often than during slavery, whites sexually harassed and even raped African-American women.

In Beaufort, South Carolina, in 1866 an employer reads the labor contract to his workers. White planters, determined to get their crops harvested, usually ignored the needs of fathers or husbands who wanted to abandon the fields in order to find their families after the war.

Freedwoman Angeline Johns once complained to a Freedmen's Bureau agent, "Mr. Humphrey beats [me] nearly every day," although she was pregnant by him and was continuing to do his "cooking, washing, and ironing." Another black woman, who had been beaten by her employer, bitterly accused him of trying "often to have intercourse with her and by reason of her obstinacy he became enraged." When he discovered that she had told her husband about his sexual advances, her employer "turned her clothes over her head & paddled her with a green fence paleing." Then, when her husband threatened to kill him for beating his wife, the employer had him arrested. Particularly during the period of Presidential Reconstruction, local courts often refused to take African-American women's complaints against white men seriously because they believed these women to be less moral than white women. Whites argued that black women's innate seductive behavior provoked the attacks, a charge the freed men and women denied.

During the days of slavery, rapes of slave women by whites generally went unpunished, but state legislatures in the South in the antebellum period passed laws prohibiting interracial marriage. This was to further ensure the inferior status of African Americans and to keep the races legally separated. In the South, interracial relationships had been without legal standing before the war, and immediately after it, the state legislatures passed new laws as part of the Black Codes to reestablish these restrictions. White Southerners especially feared having African-American men marry white women because such unions destroyed any claims whites might make to racial superiority. Later, during Congressional Reconstruction, state legislatures made up of whites and blacks repealed such laws. After Reconstruction, as segregation grew, the Southern states reinstated them.

One significant threat to the African-American family during Presidential Reconstruction was the apprenticing by whites of African-American children. In this era, state legislatures controlled by white former Confederates passed laws allowing whites to keep African-American girls until age 18 and boys until 21 without paying them or their parents for their labor. In order to remove African-American children from their parents' custody, whites were supposed to prove to the courts that the children's parents were incapable of caring for them. In Mississippi, as in other states, the law gave former slave owners

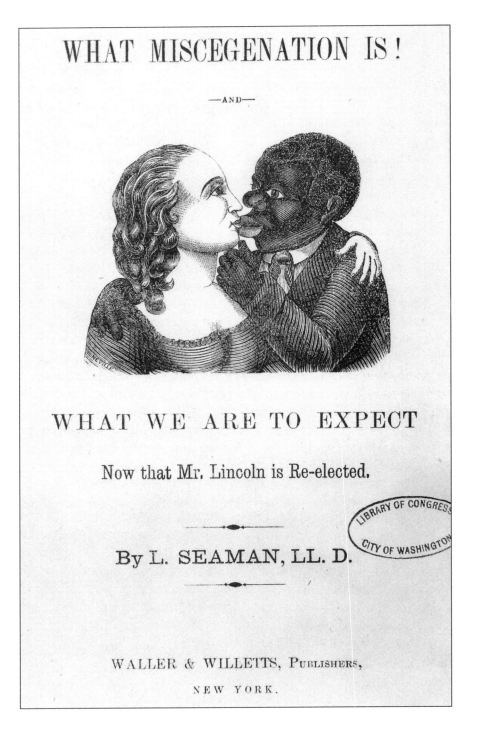

WHAT MISCEGENATION IS!

—AND—

WHAT WE ARE TO EXPECT

Now that Mr. Lincoln is Re-elected.

By L. SEAMAN, LL. D.

WALLER & WILLETTS, Publishers,

NEW YORK.

The title page of this racist book graphically illustrates white fears of miscegenation, or interracial marriage. After the war, state legislatures in the South passed laws to prohibit marriages between blacks and whites.

At left, children dressed for work as chimney sweeps in Charleston around 1866. At right, children pretend to be soldiers as they prepare for a mock battle.

preference in taking the children. Given that the courts were sympathetic to former slave owners immediately after the war and given the freed people's prevailing poverty, whites could easily convince judges of the parents' inability to provide for their children even when it was not true.

The parents of apprenticed children often went to the Freedmen's Bureau for help in getting their children back. African Americans resented the apprenticing of their children and the ongoing attempts by whites to break up their families. "I think very hard of the former owners," said one freed person, "for Trying to keep My blood when I kno that Slavery is dead." If a child's parents died, other relatives such as grandparents, aunts, uncles, brothers, and sisters would petition the bureau to gain the release of the child from apprenticeship.

Such concern for family members, whether immediate or extended family, began when children were small. After the war, freedwomen came to depend on their older children to assist in providing care for younger siblings. This was often necessary because women had to work in the fields for wages or a share of the crop even when they preferred to be with their children. Children only a couple of years older helped

watch over sisters and brothers. Freedwoman Sarah Robinson recalled, "When I got big enough I 'toted' my brother about." At 12, Rose Dowan cared for children from the time "they [were] borned and nursed them from that time up until they was large enough to care for themselves."

Knowledge of their lineage was important to African Americans so that their children would know their people. Children learned about their fathers even if they had died or were separated from their mothers

Black families sometimes lived in the same row cabins that they had occupied during slavery. These slave quarters were part of Perryclear Plantation in South Carolina.

when the children were young. According to a pension examiner who interviewed Harriet Branch, Branch's mother taught her that "her father's name was Archie Branch, and that he was a soldier and died in the U.S. service." According to Alex Henderson, "My father was Levi McLaurin I suppose. . . . I was too young to know whether my father and mother lived as husband and wife but I was always told so by my mother and grandmother."

Before and after the war, on many of the larger plantations, extended kin lived with their families. In postwar Mississippi, Suzy, an elderly former slave, resided on the same place with her three married daughters, Malenta, Nancy, and Sarah Ann, and their husbands and children. On J. A. Nixon's plantation, a freedman named Bram, who was 75, lived with his 65-year-old wife, Fanny, and his daughters, Judy and Silvy. Nixon counted Bram's granddaughter Della, Silvy's daughter, as part of Bram's family but did not mention Della's father. Nixon also listed a family that consisted of Bram's son-in-law John and his daughter Nelly. Bram's son, Jim, and his wife and baby also lived on the place, but Nixon considered them a separate family. On such plantations, children grew up with cousins as playmates and were near their grandparents, aunts, and uncles.

Extended families stayed together long after the Civil War ended. According to her testimony to a pension examiner, Caroll Russell's paternal aunt "knew him all his life." She visited him while he was stationed as a soldier in Vicksburg and "stopped one week in his house at that time." As late as 1886, most of the people living with Charlotte Branch on a plantation in Adams County, Mississippi, were her "friends . . . a number of them being relatives."

Stepfamilies, like extended families, were often relied on as part of the family network. Charlotte Brady, the daughter of Archie Branch's first wife, was sent word by Branch's widowed second wife that "she was suffering" after the war. Brady was able to arrange for her employer to send for her stepmother and have her reside on the same place. And after her slave husband enlisted in the army, Isabella Carter moved into her stepfather's house with her three children, and he continued to live near her "a great deal since the war." Half-brothers and -sisters within these families often became close. Emily Benton, who shared a birth mother with William Harris, "reared him" after the death of their

mother. Harris's wife lived with Benton "many nights while William was soldiering." When single mothers remarried, stepfathers often cared very much about their stepchildren. A freedman named Emmanuel Smith never knew his father, John Smith. Four months old when his mother began living with Albert Speers, Smith spoke affectionately of his mother's husband, saying "he is my stepfather and brought me up." And when Lucy Ann Granberry's first husband deserted her, she married Taylor Granberry. She said that Granberry was a "good father to the children and did what he could to help raise them."

After the war, women relied on relatives when they did not have a husband. Widows received help from their parents or brothers and sisters when they asked. After the death of her husband, a soldier during the war, freedwoman Helen Thomas Shaw lived with her mother and father. She recalled that "her father helped support me till he died."

Sometimes freedwomen left their husbands if they were unhappy with the treatment they received from them. Freedwoman Nettie Copper left her alcoholic and "very abusive" husband and got work taking care of a white family's children. When her husband took their 12-year-old girl, Nettie went to her father for assistance. With his help, she reclaimed her child.

Aunts and uncles played a central role in the life of William Lee, whose father and uncles had served in the army. William, his brothers and sisters, mother and aunts, and other relatives stayed at a government farm. When his mother and brothers died of measles, his aunts took him to be with his father. Then when his father died, his father's sister cared for him. Meanwhile, his uncle, Robert Lee, finished his army service and returned to the plantation where the family had lived as slaves. When Robert Lee learned about his brother's death in 1867, he sent for William and his sister to live with him. William "returned to the vicinity of his old home . . . and he has lived in said vicinity ever since," for at least 12 years, according to his uncle.

Being part of an extended family meant that people cared for their elderly relatives when they were able to. Aged former slaves discovered that finding jobs after the war was difficult. Employers hired only the most physically fit men and women to do agricultural labor. Worn out from slavery, the elderly were forced to depend on their children and other family members to provide for them. Freed people tried to support their parents, but given their own poverty, found it difficult. Immediately after the war, when freed people needed help, they turned to the Freedmen's Bureau. The Bureau was reluctant to incur the cost of providing for aging former slaves, but it did build hospitals for the freed people. When necessary, it transported the destitute or sick to medical facilities.

Local governments, particularly those under Democratic control, resisted taking responsibility for older former slaves unable to work. Even though African Americans paid taxes, local municipalities refused to provide services for blacks in need. During Presidential Reconstruction, local governments passed specific "pauper" taxes, which only African Americans had to pay, but whites still continued to claim that they could not provide assistance to African Americans. However, during Congressional Reconstruction, more hospitals and orphanages were built, due in part to the lobbying by African-American lawmakers.

Families of freed people in the South showed both continuity and change from the days of slavery. As with slave families, the extended

Many of the people gathered for this group photo in the 1890s are probably related. Extended families tended to stay together after the war, sharing the burdens of caring for the children, the elderly, and the sick.

A "Freedmen's Village" grew up in Arlington Heights, Virginia, after the war. Although the Freedmen's Bureau could not take responsibility for all ex-slaves in need, it did build hospitals and schools and offered many essential services.

family continued to play an important part in people's lives. Unfortunately, white denigration of the male role in the black family and whites' sexual abuse of African-American women carried over from slavery. The practice of whites' apprenticing freed people's children also affected family unity. These issues all stemmed from attempts by white Southerners to establish their racial domination after the war. Even though whites did not fully recognize freed people's right to make decisions for their own families, African Americans were able to exercise much more control over their family life than they had been able to as slaves. Men became the legal heads of their households, and men and women alike were able to raise their children without constant white intervention. Racial oppression failed to extinguish the strength of African-American families during Reconstruction.

CHAPTER 6

COMMUNITY: "IT WAS A WHOLE RACE TRYING TO GO TO SCHOOL"

◇ ◇ ◇

During the Civil War, the Reverend William H. Hunter, a chaplain in the U.S. Army, returned to North Carolina, where he had been a slave, and preached the following sermon.

A few short years ago I left North Carolina a slave. I now return a man. I have the honor to be a regular minister of the Gospel in the Methodist Episcopal Church of the United States and also a regularly commissioned chaplain in the American Army. . . . I am proud to inform you that just three weeks ago today, as black a man as you ever saw, preached in the city of Washington to the Congress of the United States; and that a short time ago another colored man was admitted to the bar of the Supreme Court of the United States as a lawyer. One week ago you were all slaves; now you are all free.

Hunter, like many freed people, saw the Civil War in religious terms: "Thank God the armies of the Lord and of Gideon has triumphed and the Rebels have been driven back in confusion and scattered like chaff before the wind."

The political nature of Hunter's sermon is representative of others during Reconstruction, for community activities within the church served as a power base for African-American leadership. Throughout the country, barriers against African Americans' full participation in U.S. society began to fall during Reconstruction, as blacks struggled during and after

The Freedmen's Bureau operated this North Carolina school. In addition to white teachers, many Northern blacks traveled to the South in order to teach the newly freed slaves.

the war to achieve equal rights in both the South and the North. They also formed their own organizations such as churches, schools, and social clubs.

These new institutions took the place of the slave communities that were then breaking up on the plantations. As sharecropping developed, freed people gradually moved out of their old slave quarters—rows of cabins, often attached to each other—and into individual cabins built on the land on which they worked. Workers usually rented these places. While no longer in the close living quarters of slavery, freed people continued to socialize. Weekends, particularly Saturday night and Sunday, and holidays were a perfect time to get together. Friends and neighbors gathered at church services, weddings, and funerals. In 1867, for example, when James Johnson married Martha Johnson, who lived on a neighboring plantation, approximately 50 people from the two plantations attended.

Conversation was the most popular form of entertainment on the plantation. Everyone discussed other people's private business, particularly the details of their love lives. After the war, as freedman Albert Duball observed, "Such things are generally known when a woman lives with a man and is not married." Information was also shared about work, including crop yields and prices and who paid the most. Freed people kept each other informed about Ku Klux Klan activities or other organized violence in the area to try to protect each other.

During slavery, women had worked together in field gangs, but this became less common after the war. With sharecropping, women were brought together less often by work, but they continued to depend on each other during special circumstances such as childbirth. Midwives (women who deliver babies) cared for both the babies and the mothers. After one midwife, Rena Clarke, washed and dressed a baby, she "would tie a mole's right foot around his neck" in order to ensure "good health. . . . and good luck." For colic, Clarke recommended "a mixture of soot and sugar from the tenth brick of the chimney." A small pouch of asafetida (from the carrot family) worn around the neck was thought to prevent measles, mumps, and other childhood illnesses. If a midwife was unavailable, other women attended during childbirth. As women aided each other during the birth of the child, they also tended each other at the end of life. One freedwoman recalled, "I was present when Rhoda was on her death bed and waited on her." Women confided in each other when they fell in love or had trouble with their men. Mary Jordan recalled that Rosa Duncan, upset because her husband had other women, "talked to me many times about how Joe Duncan had treated her."

Such closeness did not mean the absence of tension among African Americans, however. Most complaints brought to the Freedmen's Bureau were about white employers not paying their workers, but occasionally freed people brought grievances against one another. Occasionally, an African-American employer did not pay his employees, or lack of fencing sometimes caused friction when a mule or cow invaded a neighbor's garden. In one ongoing conflict, Rebecca Flournoy and Anderson Forrister quarreled because Flournoy continually allowed her mule to run through his crops until one day Forrister kicked the mule, which caused Flournoy to become furious. She called Forrister "a low lived dirty dog." According to Forrister, Flournoy then struck him over the head with a stick. She in turn accused him of hitting her with an axe

These women near Beaufort, South Carolina, were excused from work to take care of their children. As in slavery, women continued to depend on each other for help and companionship as they reared their children.

handle. African-American women also argued with each other over family concerns. Quarrels sometimes started over children and husbands. In one case, freedwoman Mary Jane Royal argued with both her husband and Lizzie Jones over an affair he was having with Jones.

Conflict between individuals did not keep freed people from working toward common goals, such as education for themselves and their children. Education fulfilled practical needs, such as being able to read labor contracts, and it increased the possibility of the next generation's upward mobility. As one freedman said, "I wishes the Children all in School. it is better for them then to be their Serveing a mistes." Another one pronounced: "If I nebber does do nothing more while I live, I shall give my children a chance to go school, for I considers education next best thing to liberty." Being educated was also a way to counter the racist myth that African Americans were innately intellectually inferior to whites.

During the war, many freed people received their first formal lessons from Northern teachers who visited army and contraband camps. One teacher commented on soldiers stationed in Vicksburg: "I have taught in the North...and have never seen such zeal on the part of pupils, nor such advancement as I see here." Education was as important to black soldiers as their freedom. One soldier proudly declared, "A large portion of the regiment have been going to school during the winter months. Surely this is a mighty and progressive age in which we live."

Groups such as the American Missionary Association arranged for teachers to travel south to instruct both soldiers and civilians. Charlotte Forten, an African American from Philadelphia whose relatives were prominent abolitionists, taught former slave children during the war on the Sea Islands off the coast of South Carolina. She wrote in her journal: "I enjoyed it much. The children are well-behaved and eager to learn. It will be a happiness to teach them." Besides instructing her students in the fundamentals of reading and writing, she taught history, such as the overthrow of French rule in Haiti led by the Haitian Toussaint L'Ouverture. Forten "talked to the children a little while to-day about the noble Toussaint. They listened very attentively. It is well that they sh'ld know what one of their own color c'ld do for his race. I long to inspire them with courage and ambition (of a noble sort) and high purpose."

White women civilians stand behind the black soldiers they taught to read and write during the war. Some of the soldiers hold open books in their laps.

Northern teachers set up makeshift schools on plantations that were under Union control. Southern planters and the Northerners leasing plantations were unenthusiastic about any educational efforts, fearing they would interfere with their disciplining of the labor force. During and after the war, freed people established their own schools. Sometimes they received help from the Freedmen's Bureau or Northern societies set up to aid the newly freed slaves, but they also opened schools without outside assistance. As a freedwoman in Alabama pointed out proudly, "Whoever may hereafter lay acclaim to the honor of 'establishing' . . . schools, I trust the fact will never be ignored that Miss Lucy Lee, one of the emancipated, was the pioneer teacher of the colored children . . . without the aid of Northern societies." African Americans usually ended up paying for their own teachers and school buildings, even though they often tried to include provisions in their labor contracts stipulating that their employers would provide the schools.

Along with primary schools, during Reconstruction institutions of higher education for African Americans were also founded. Among these were Howard University, Fisk University, Atlanta University, Clark University, Alcorn State University, Bethune-Cookman College, Hampton Institute, and Richmond Theological Seminary. Many of these institutions were founded as teachers' colleges to train African Americans as educators, although they also taught other job skills.

After the war, the Freedmen's Bureau established 740 schools with more than 1,000 white and African-American teachers. More significantly, during Congressional Reconstruction, under pressure from blacks, Southern states developed school systems financed by public rather than private funds. Throughout the South, schools of whatever sort were segregated, although African Americans made attempts to integrate them.

While children attended schools during the day, adults went to night school after a full day of work. As the African American educator Booker T. Washington explained, "Few people who were not right in the

The main building of Howard University in Washington, D.C., in 1870. Founded only three years earlier, Howard was one of several black colleges established after the war that provided professional training.

In 1873, the Jubilee Singers traveled to New York from Fisk University in Nashville, Tennessee, to give a benefit concert. As they raised money, the singers introduced black spirituals to new audiences in the North.

midst of the scenes can form any exact idea of the intense desire which the people of my race showed for education. It was a whole race trying to go to school. Few were too young, and none too old, to make the attempt to learn." At one school in Atlanta, for example, children attended school until 2:00 in the afternoon, followed by adults; evening classes were held until 10:00 at night. "The parents are delighted with the idea of their children learning to read, and many take great pleasure in visiting the schools," one educator reported, "and asking the teacher to pay 'ticular pains to our children, as we wish them to get all the learning they can, 'caus you know Miss, I's got no learning myself consequently I know how much I loses without it."

Many Southern whites remained distinctly hostile to formal education for African Americans. Resentful about being taxed to pay for their education, whites were afraid that once blacks gained an education, they would fight white supremacy with even greater determination. Planters typically preferred black children to work in the fields rather than attend school. They feared that once their laborers gained an education, they would refuse field work and domestic service in favor of higher-paying jobs with better working conditions.

Because white Southerners refused to rent rooms to Northern teachers of African-American students, the teachers often had trouble finding places to live. Local whites, including the members of the Ku Klux Klan, sometimes threatened teachers, forcing them to leave. Also, whites often resisted former slaves' attempts to buy land to build schools. Occasionally, they took the extreme measure of burning down African-American schools, or they destroyed books. One Klansman "dar[ed] any other n——r to have a book in his house." Other, more moderate, whites encouraged the establishment of segregated schools to avoid the possibility of integration.

The desire for education for their children and more autonomy in the workplace caused thousands of rural African Americans to leave their plantations and go north and west or into Southern cities. Oppressive economic, social, and political conditions in the South caused thousands of African Americans to go west, particularly in the late Reconstruction period. The West seemed to promise fewer racial restrictions and more opportunities, although before the war, many western territories had restricted the settlement of free African Americans. In the Wyoming territories, however, African-American men were allowed to vote.

During Reconstruction, African Americans achieved some measure of equality, aided by a coalition of white Republicans. In the North and West, blacks utilized the civil rights acts passed by Congress to end discrimination and gain access to public facilities. In the West, even though their numbers were small, African Americans agitated for equality during

A street fight between black and white students in New Orleans in 1875, after white boys had raided an integrated school. Following the example of their parents, many white children fought against blacks receiving an equal education.

Nat Love, who worked as a cowpuncher out West, used the skills he had learned as a slave on a Texas ranch. African Americans went west looking for both economic opportunities and freedom from racial oppression.

Reconstruction. Under the influence of the dominant Republican party, legalized discrimination diminished in the West. Minnesota and Iowa granted suffrage to African-American men even before the ratification of the 15th Amendment. In 1865, Illinois and Ohio repealed many of their discriminatory laws, including those prohibiting blacks from serving on juries. In California, African Americans began a petition drive to support the right of black men to testify in court, which was granted in 1863. Several western states started to desegregate their streetcars. In San Francisco, as elsewhere, transportation was desegregated, but some public facilities were segregated and restricted seating to separate areas.

African-American political involvement grew noticeably after the 15th Amendment was ratified. In the West, as in the South, blacks were overwhelmingly Republican. In Detroit, men formed the Lincoln Sixth Ward Republican Club, and blacks later ran for public office there with only limited success. In Colorado, African-American men served as delegates to Republican conventions.

African-American communities grew in the West, despite their small populations. California contained the largest number of African Americans in the Far West—more than 4,000. In the Midwest, more than 17,000 blacks lived in Kansas, far more than in any other western state. There were some 600 African-American ministers in the West, about 200 in Kansas alone. In 1864 an African Methodist church was formed in Carson City, Nevada, even though the entire population of blacks in the whole state was only 367. Fraternal and social clubs and newspapers were all started, and San Francisco had two African-American newspaper editors.

Reconstruction also had an impact on the Northern African-American population as well as on blacks in the South and West. African Americans made up less than 2 percent of the population in the North,

but they had long agitated there for equal rights. In Massachusetts, African Americans integrated various public places for the first time. In 1867, Philadelphia allowed African Americans to sit with whites on streetcars. However, only with the passage of the 15th Amendment could African-American men vote throughout the North. And once they were able to vote, their small proportion in the overall population made it difficult for them to achieve significant political power. As a result, very few Northern African-American men were elected to office.

As opposed to the South, where only New Orleans allowed white and African-American children to attend school together, several states in the West and North desegregated their public school systems. Rhode

African Americans in the West frequently worked as manual laborers—helping to build railroads, for example. These workers in Colorado haul a load of hay.

Island in 1866 and Connecticut in 1868 allowed white and African-American children to go to school together. In many large cities, such as Chicago, black children were educated alongside whites. Michigan desegregated its schools in 1867, although the Detroit school board did not comply until 1871. African-American parents protested that the board had earlier ignored the desegregation ruling, and their activism helped persuade it to end the practice of having separate schools. In the 1870s, Nevada and Oregon allowed integrated schools, and in San Francisco, blacks met and passed resolutions opposing separate schools. The state courts there ruled that schools could be separate but they must have equal facilities. In 1875, the segregated schools were abolished in San Francisco. The measure passed in part as a response to the declining economy of the 1870s, which made maintaining separate school systems more difficult.

In the North, African Americans gained access to state-funded colleges that had previously denied them admission. Discrimination continued to be a problem there, however. In Cincinnati, one African

Students from an integrated school in New Orleans. Although some western and northern cities allowed integrated schools after the war, in the South only New Orleans approved such an arrangement.

American pointed out that racism "hampers me in every relation of life, in business, in politics, in religion, as a father or as a husband."

Along with moving to the North and West, African Americans also settled in Southern cities in an attempt to find freedom. In the five-year period after the war, the African-American population doubled in several Southern cities. Violence on the plantations was part of what motivated blacks to move to the cities. As one African-American state representative pointed out, "People who get scared at others being beaten go to the cities." In the cities, African Americans joined newly established churches, voluntary associations such as burial societies (which insured funds for funerals), savings and loan associations, and clubs—both social and political—established by and for African Americans. Lodges such as the Colored Masons and Colored Odd Fellows were founded. Blacks also formed their own volunteer fire companies such as the Victor Engine Company and the Bucket and Ladder Company in Raleigh, North Carolina, in part because Southern whites refused to integrate those already in existence. The state militia also developed all-black units. In Southern

As African Americans adapted to life after slavery, they formed their own churches, social and political clubs, and other associations. These men in Richmond, Virginia, were members of the Astoria Beneficial Club.

Love and Union

Members of the Neptune Volunteer Fire Company in Greenville, South Carolina. When whites in the South refused to integrate such organizations, blacks established their own.

cities, African Americans lived in areas that became increasingly segregated from whites, in substandard housing, often at the edge of town.

Southern cities did not offer an escape from unequal treatment. Occasional outbreaks of violence, including rioting against African Americans in Memphis and New Orleans in 1866, made blacks wary. Public facilities were usually segregated, with African Americans rarely receiving the same level of service or accommodations as whites. Theaters allowed African Americans to attend, but let them sit only in certain sections, often those with the least desirable seats. Some places, such as the New Orleans Opera House, that did not racially segregate people often openly refused admittance to African Americans. In many cities—including Charleston, New Orleans, Richmond, Mobile, Nashville, Louisville, and Savannah—African Americans organized campaigns to integrate streetcars but had limited success. Often, they had to settle for segregated cars.

Both in the cities and in rural areas after the war, freed people established their own places to worship. Those who as slaves had gone with their masters to church services and listened to white preachers exhort them to be obedient to their masters now organized churches independent and separate from those of whites. To this effort, blacks throughout the South gave their money. For example, in Charleston, South Carolina, by 1866 African Americans had established 11 churches. White churches became increasingly segregated as whites refused to integrate their facilities or allow blacks to hold leadership roles. In rural areas, freed people attended church services in cabins or held outside prayer meetings away from their former masters and other whites. Most blacks gravitated to African-American controlled Baptist churches, but others joined the African Methodist Episcopal Church. In certain parts of the South, particularly in New Orleans, African Americans practiced Catholicism.

Churches forged vital links within the freed African American community. Particularly in the cities, attendance was so great that churches often offered three, rather than the normal two, services on Sunday. Services sometimes lasted two hours, during which ministers read letters from former slaves wanting to know about family members separated during slavery. Church buildings also provided school classrooms and places for meetings and lectures. And social life often centered around the church. Laura Ford met her future husband "at a meetin' one Sunday" at church.

Entire religious communities encouraged and celebrated the individual's salvation, which brought a person into the religious congregation. One freed girl informed her white teacher: "Ann's come through. And she's shouted for three days, an' she can't hold her baby she's dat full o' glory, she don' eat a bit." When the teacher visited Ann, who was still repeating "glory, glory," the teacher was impressed by the placid look on Ann's face and interpreted it as a sign of inner peace with God. The teacher reported that "from the quarters came a shout of 'Hallelujah. Ann's cum through.'"

African Americans also celebrated official membership in the church together. "Saw a wonderful sight to-day, 150 people were baptized in the creek near the church," remarked Charlotte Forten. "They looked very picturesque—many of them in white aprons, and bright dresses and handkerchiefs. And as they, in procession, marched down to the water, they sang beautifully. The most perfect order and quiet prevailed throughout."

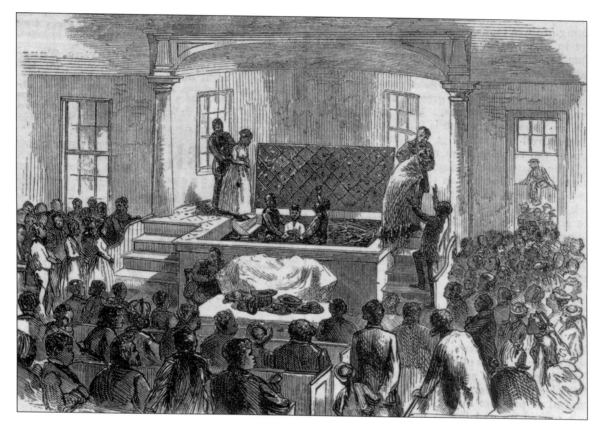

Members of the congregation are baptized at the First African Baptist Church in Richmond, Virginia. Such churches became the hub of social, political, and educational activities as well as religious ones.

Religion also played a role in encouraging education. Because many freed people held deeply felt religious convictions, wanting to read the Bible provided them with another strong incentive to learn to read. One Northern teacher recalled an elderly freedwoman who "came to me the other evening asking me to teach her how to read; she said she wanted to learn how, that her mind might be fixed on things higher and nobler than things of this world, and if she could read the Bible, it would be a great source of happiness to her."

During Reconstruction, freed people used the church—the African-American institution least controlled by whites—to promote political participation. Ministers freely mixed religion with political activism. As one religious leader in Florida explained, "A man in this State cannot do his whole duty as a minister except he looks out for political interests of his people." During Reconstruction, more than 100 ministers served in Southern state legislatures. Involvement with the church for

both the clergy and lay officials as with organizing schools and burial and fraternal societies gave African-American men experience as leaders within their own institutions and helped train them to become effective politicians.

As with religion, whole communities of African Americans partici- pated in political events. Loyal Leagues, formed to support the Republican party, held social gatherings including dances. In at least one Mississippi community, freed people gathered at the church and walked together to local polling places. Women and children marched with the men voters in these parades.

Politics was important to the entire community of African Ameri- cans. Freed people often thought of the vote as belonging to the community of freed people rather than to just one person. African-American women, like the men, hoped that having black men vote would ensure a redistribution of land, better schools, equal opportu-

Black men vote in Virginia in November 1871. African Ameri- cans hoped that by exercising their right to vote, they could restructure their com- munities and guaran- tee for themselves equal opportunities.

nity for jobs, and equal access to public facilities. African-American men voted overwhelmingly for the Republican party, sometimes with a turnout as high as 90 percent, and African-American women supported their men's decisions. As one Northern teacher described the scene at a polling place, "The colored women formed a line of one hundred or more, and ran up and down near the line of voters, saying . . . 'Now Jack, ef you don' vote for Lincum's men I'll leave ye.'" Planters complained that their field laborers left work to attend political rallies. In Richmond, Virginia, during the Republican state convention, the owners of tobacco factories had to shut down because so many of their African-American workers had gone to the convention.

During Reconstruction, the old, tightly knit slave communities on the larger plantations began to disperse, especially with the spread of family sharecropping and the building of separate cabins. After the war, a sense of having shared interests and goals strengthened collective efforts in education, religion, and politics, widening freed people's vision of the meaning of community. Despite fierce white opposition that included violence, African Americans persevered to establish their own churches and schools.

Resisting intense hostility, African Americans participated in America's political life through meetings, conventions, protests for the integration of public facilities, and voting. Even with the ultimate failure of Reconstruction and the return of Democratic party rule, the new autonomy compared favorably to slavery, and African-American families, churches, and schools endured to provide a lasting legacy.

Appendix:
Civil Rights Amendments to the Constitution

13th Amendment (ratified Dec. 6, 1865)

1. Neither slavery nor involuntary servitude, except as a punishment for crime whereof the party shall have been duly convicted, shall exist within the United States, or any place subject to their jurisdiction.

2. Congress shall have power to enforce this article by appropriate legislation.

14th Amendment (ratified July 9, 1868)

1. All persons born or naturalized in the United States, and subject to the jurisdiction thereof, are citizens of the United States and of the State wherein they reside. No State shall make or enforce any law which shall abridge the privileges or immunities of citizens of the United States; nor shall any State deprive any person of life, liberty, or property, without due process of law; nor deny to any person within its jurisdiction the equal protection of the laws.

2. Representatives shall be apportioned among the several States according to their respective numbers, counting the whole number of persons in each State, excluding Indians not taxed. But when the right to vote at any election for the choice of electors for President and Vice-President of the United States, Representatives in Congress, the Executive and Judicial officers of a State, or the members of the Legislature thereof, is denied to any of the male inhabitants of such State, being twenty-one years of age, and citizens of the United Sates, or in any way abridged, except for participation in rebellion, or other crime, the basis of representation therein shall be reduced in the proportion which the number of such male citizens shall bear to the whole number of male citizens twenty-one years of age in such State.

3. No person shall be a Senator or Representative in Congress, or elector of President and Vice-President, or hold any office, civil or military, under the United Sates, or under any State, who, having previously taken an oath, as a member of Congress, or as an officer of the United States, or as a member of any State legislature, or as an executive or judicial officer of any State, to support the Constitution of the United Sates, shall have engaged in insurrection or rebellion against the same, or given aid or comfort to the enemies thereof. But Congress may, by a vote of two-thirds of each house, remove such disability.

4. The validity of the public debt of the United Sates, authorized by law, including debts incurred for payment of pensions and bounties for services in suppressing insurrection or rebellion, shall not be questioned. But neither the United Sates nor any State shall assume or pay any debt or obligation incurred in aid of insurrection or rebellion against the United Sates, or any claim for the loss or emancipation of any slave; but all such debts, obligations, and claims shall be held illegal and void.

5. The Congress shall have power to enforce, by appropriate legislation, the provisions of this article.

15th Amendment (ratified Feb. 3, 1870)

1. The right of citizens of the United Sates to vote shall not be denied or abridged by the United States or by any State on account of race, color, or previous condition of servitude.

2. The Congress shall have power to enforce this article by appropriate legislation.

CHRONOLOGY

1861
Eleven states secede and organize the Confederate States of America.

APRIL 12, 1861
Confederate firing on Fort Sumter, South Carolina, begins the Civil War.

AUGUST 6, 1861
First Confiscation Act prevents slave owners from reenslaving runaways.

APRIL 16, 1862
Slavery is abolished in Washington, D.C.

JULY 17, 1862
Congress permits the enlistment of black soldiers.

JANUARY 1, 1863
Lincoln's Emancipation Proclamation goes into effect.

JULY 13, 1863
Draft riots begin in New York.

APRIL 12, 1864
Fort Pillow, Tennessee, massacre of Union soldiers, including blacks.

JUNE 15, 1864
Congress approves equal pay to African-American soldiers.

MARCH 3, 1865
Congress establishes Bureau of Refugees, Freedmen, and Abandoned Lands.

APRIL 9, 1865
General Robert E. Lee surrenders to General Ulysses S. Grant at the town of Appomattox Court House, Virginia.

APRIL 14, 1965
Lincoln is assassinated. Vice President Andrew Johnson becomes President.

DECEMBER 6, 1865
13th Amendment, abolishing slavery, is adopted.

APRIL 1, 1866
First national Ku Klux Klan convention.

APRIL 9, 1866
Congress passes Civil Rights Bill.

1868
President Andrew Johnson is impeached by the House of Representatives, but the Senate votes not to remove him from office.

Ulysses S. Grant is elected President.

JULY 9, 1868
14th Amendment, granting citizenship to freed people, is adopted.

FEBRUARY 3, 1870
15th Amendment, granting freedmen but not women the right to vote, is ratified.

FEBRUARY 25, 1870
Hiram Revels of Mississippi is elected to the U.S. Senate and takes the seat once held by Jefferson Davis.

1872
Ulysses S. Grant is reelected President.

DECEMBER 11, 1872
Pinckney B. S. Pinchback becomes governor of Louisiana.

MARCH 1, 1875
Congress passes Civil Rights Act.

1877
Rutherford B. Hayes becomes President with agreement to remove federal troops from the South.

FURTHER READING

◇ ◇ ◇

A NOTE ON SOURCES

The primary sources consulted for this book include interviews with former slaves collected in the 1930s by the Works Progress Administration. Another source was the collection of Civil War widows' pension files (for the United States Colored Troops, as they were designated). Pension examiners recorded testimony from former slaves to determine who deserved a pension. Reminiscences of war experiences and family matters appear in these documents. The Freedmen's Bureau records provided a third source of material. These documents from the 1860s include labor contracts, complaints brought by freed people to bureau agents, and reports on Freedmen's Bureau schools and hospitals. They also contain letters from African-American Union soldiers during the Civil War.

In the interest of readability, the volumes in this series include no discussion of historiography and no footnotes. As works of synthesis and overview, however, they are greatly indebted to the research and writing of other historians. The principal works drawn on in this volume are among the books listed below.

GENERAL AFRICAN-AMERICAN HISTORIES

Anderson, James D. *The Education of Blacks in the South, 1860–1935.* Chapel Hill: University of North Carolina Press, 1988.

Bennett, Lerone, Jr. *Before the Mayflower: A History of Black America.* 6th rev. ed. New York: Viking Penguin, 1988.

————. *The Shaping of Black America.* New York: Viking Penguin, 1993.

Daniels, Douglas Henry. *Pioneer Urbanites: A Social and Cultural History of Black San Francisco.* Philadelphia: Temple University Press, 1980.

Foner, Philip S. *History of Black Americans: From Africa to the Emergence of the Cotton Kingdom.* Westport, Conn.: Greenwood, 1975.

Franklin, John H., and Alfred A. Moss, Jr. *From Slavery to Freedom: A History of Negro Americans.* 6th ed. New York: Knopf, 1987.

Gates, Henry L., Jr. *A Chronology of African-American History from 1445–1980.* New York: Amistad, 1980.

Giddings, Paula. *When and Where I Enter: The Impact of Black Women on Race and Sex in America.* New York: Bantam, 1985.

Gutman, Herbert G. *The Black Family in Slavery and Freedom, 1750–1925.* New York: Vintage, 1977.

Harding, Vincent. *There Is a River: The Black Struggle for Freedom in America.* San Diego: Harcourt Brace, 1981.

Hine, Darlene C., et al., eds. *Black Women in America.* Brooklyn, N.Y.: Carlson, 1993.

Hornsby, Alton, Jr. *Chronology of African-American History: Significant Events and People from 1619 to the Present.* Detroit: Gale Research, 1991.

Jones, Jacqueline. *Labor of Love, Labor of Sorrow: Black Women, Work, and the Family, from Slavery to the Present.* New York: Vintage, 1985.

Litwack, Leon, and August Meier. *Black Leaders of the 19th Century.* Urbana: University of Illinois Press, 1988.

Meltzer, Milton. *The Black Americans: A History in Their Own Words.* Rev. ed. New York: HarperCollins, 1984.

Mintz, Sidney W., and Richard Price. *The Birth of African-American Culture: An Anthropological Perspective.* Boston: Beacon Press, 1992.

Savage, William Sherman. *Blacks in the West.* Westport, Conn.: Greenwood Press, 1976.

Quarles, Benjamin. *The Negro in the Making of America.* 3rd ed. New York: Macmillan, 1987.

GENERAL CIVIL WAR HISTORIES

Foner, Eric. *Reconstruction: America's Unfinished Revolution, 1863–1877.* New York: Harper & Row, 1988.

Franklin, John Hope. *Reconstruction after the Civil War.* Chicago: University of Chicago Press, 1961.

McPherson, James M. *Battle Cry of Freedom: The Civil War Era.* New York: Oxford University Press, 1988.

HISTORIES OF AFRICAN AMERICANS DURING THE CIVIL WAR ERA

Bardaglio, Peter. "The Children of Jubilee: African American Childhood in Wartime." In *Divided Houses: Gender and the Civil War,* edited by Catherine Clinton and Nina Silber. New York: Oxford University Press, 1992.

Berlin, Ira, et. al. *Free At Last: A Documentary History of Slavery, Freedom, and the Civil War.* New York: The New Press, 1992.

Billington, Ray Allen, ed. *The Journal of Charlotte L. Forten: A Free Negro in the Slave Era.* London: Collier-Macmillan, 1961.

Davis, Ronald L. F. *Good and Faithful Labor: From Slavery to Sharecropping in the Natchez District, 1860–1890.* Westport, Conn.: Greenwood Press, 1982.

Du Bois, William E. B. *Black Reconstruction in America, 1860–1880.* New York: Atheneum, 1962.

Foner, Eric. *Freedom's Lawmakers: A Directory of Black Officeholders During Reconstruction.* New York: Oxford University Press, 1993.

Gerteis, Louis S. *From Contraband to Freedman: Federal Policy toward Southern Blacks, 1861–1865.* Westport, Conn.: Greenwood Press, 1973.

Glatthaar, Joseph I. *Forged in Battle: The Civil Alliance of Black Soldiers and White Officers.* New York: Free Press, 1990.

Holt, Thomas. *Black over White: Negro Political Leadership in South Carolina during Reconstruction.* Urbana: University of Illinois Press, 1977.

Horton, James Oliver, and Lois E. Horton. *Black Bostonians: Family Life and Community Struggle in the Antebellum North.* New York: Holmes & Meier, 1979.

Jaynes, Gerald David. *Branches Without Roots: Genesis of the Black Working Class in the American South, 1862–1882.* New York: Oxford University Press, 1986.

Katzman, David M. *Before the Ghetto: Black Detroit in the Nineteenth Century.* Urbana: University of Illinois Press, 1973.

Kolchin, Peter. *First Freedom: The Responses of Alabama's Blacks to Emancipation and Reconstruction.* Westport, Conn.: Greenwood Press, 1972.

Leckie, William H. *The Buffalo Soldiers: A Narrative of the Negro Cavalry in the West.* Norman: University of Oklahoma Press, 1967.

Litwack, Leon E. *Been in the Storm So Long: The Aftermath of Slavery.* New York: Knopf, 1979.

McPherson, James M. *Marching toward Freedom: Blacks in the Civil War, 1861–1865.* New York: Facts on File, 1991.

————. *The Negro's Civil War: How American Negroes Felt and Acted during the War for the Union.* New York: Vintage, 1965.

Miller, Edward A. *Gullah Statesman: Robert Smalls from Slavery to Congress, 1839–1915.* Columbia: University of South Carolina Press, 1995.

Mohr, Clarence L. *On the Threshold of Freedom: Masters and Slaves in Civil War Georgia.* Athens: University of Georgia Press, 1886.

Pearson, Elizabeth Ware. *Letters from Port Royal, 1862–1868.* New York: Arno Press and the *New York Times*, 1969.

Quarles, Benjamin. *The Negro in the Civil War.* Boston: Little, Brown, 1969.

Rabinowitz, Howard N. *Race Relations in the Urban South, 1865–1890.* New York: Oxford University Press, 1978.

Ransom, Robert L., and Richard Sutch. *One Kind of Freedom: The Economic Consequences of Emancipation.* New York: Cambridge University Press, 1977.

Rawich, George P. *The American Slave: A Composite Autobiography.* Westport, Conn.: Greenwood Press, 1972.

INDEX

◇ ◇ ◇

ACKNOWLEDGMENTS

◇ ◇ ◇

I want to thank Earl Lewis and Robin Kelley for asking me to contribute to their important project and for their helpful suggestions on the manuscript. The Oxford staff, particularly Nancy Toff, Tara Deal, and Lisa Kirchner, have been superb. I thank my family, William and Elizabeth Kost and Herbert and Malvina Frankel, for their encouragement and vast resources of good humor. Lastly, the cats' company while I wrote was very much appreciated.

PICTURE CREDITS

◇ ◇ ◇

NORALEE FRANKEL ◇ ◇ ◇

Noralee Frankel is Assistant Director on Women and Minorities at the American Historical Association. She is the coeditor of *Gender, Class, Race, and Reform in the Progressive Era* and author of the forthcoming *Freedom's Women: Black Women in Mississippi in the Civil War Era*. In addition, she has published various articles dealing with the issues of race and gender.

ROBIN D. G. KELLEY ◇ ◇ ◇

Robin D. G. Kelley is professor of history and Africana studies at New York University. He previously taught history and African-American studies at the University of Michigan. He is the author of *Hammer and Hoe: Alabama Communists during the Great Depression,* which received the Eliot Rudwick Prize of the Organization of American Historians and was named Outstanding Book on Human Rights by the Gustavus Myers Center for the Study of Human Rights in the United States. Professor Kelley is also the author of *Race Rebels: Culture, Politics, and the Black Working Class* and coeditor of *Imagining Home: Class, Culture, and Nationalism in the African Diaspora.*

EARL LEWIS ◇ ◇ ◇

Earl Lewis is professor of history and Afroamerican studies at the University of Michigan. He served as director of the university's Center for Afroamerican and African Studies from 1990 to 1993. Professor Lewis is the author of *In Their Own Interests: Race, Class and Power in Twentieth Century Norfolk* and coauthor of *Blacks in the Industrial Age: A Documentary History.*